Bringing Innovation to Market

BRADFORD
COLLEGE
LIBRARY

Bringing Innovation to Market

How to Break Corporate and Customer Barriers

JAGDISH N. SHETH
School of Business Administration
University of Southern California
Los Angeles, California

S. RAM
College of Business
& Public Administration
University of Arizona
Tucson, Arizona

JOHN WILEY & SONS
New York • Chichester • Brisbane • Toronto • Singapore

Copyright © 1987 by Jagdish N. Sheth and S. Ram
Published by John Wiley & Sons, Inc.

All rights reserved. Published simultaneously in Canada.

Reproduction or translation of any part of this work beyond that permitted by Section 107 or 108 of the 1976 United States Copyright Act without the permission of the copyright owner is unlawful. Requests for permission or further information should be addressed to the Permissions Department, John Wiley & Sons, Inc.

This publication is designed to provide accurate and authoritative information in regard to the subject matter covered. It is sold with the understanding that the publisher is not engaged in rendering legal, accounting, or other professional service. If legal advice or other expert assistance is required, the services of a competent professional person should be sought. *From a Declaration of Principles jointly adopted by a Committee of the American Bar Association and a Committee of Publishers.*

Library of Congress Cataloging in Publication Data

   (Wiley management series on problem solving, decision making, and strategic thinking)
     Includes index.

Sheth, Jagdish N.
   Bringing innovation to market: how to break corporate and customer barriers / Jagdish N. Sheth, S. Ram.
     p.   cm.
   Bibliography: p.
   Includes index.
   ISBN 0-471-84977-4
    1. New products. 2. Technological innovations. I. Ram, S. (Sundaresan), 1957–   II. Title.
HD69.N4S494 1987
658.5'78—dc19   87–17611
                                       CIP

ISBN 0-471-84977-4

Printed in the United States of America
10 9 8 7 6 5 4 3 2 1

*In memory of my father,
who knew how to overcome
business barriers*
(J.S.)

This Book Is Dedicated to
*Sudha Ram, my wife,
for her constant encouragement
and enthusiasm*
(S.R.)

Preface

The freedom to experiment and innovate has undoubtedly enabled the United States to become a leading nation in the world. Innovations have allowed us to expand to our geographic, scientific, and business frontiers. Innovations have consistently bettered our lot. They reduce the fatigue in our daily routine, save us time, and save us money. They create opportunities for profitable commercial enterprise, encourage competition, and provide impetus to economic growth. Today, we are in the midst of a technological revolution that promises dramatic innovations such as controlled genetic evolution and machines that can think.

While innovations have thus been beneficial to mankind, historical evidence suggests that the path of innovating is strewn with thorns. Innovations have consistently met with resistance. The steam engine was shunned initially, and airplanes were first considered evil magic for defying gravity. Currently, we are witnessing resistance to innovative videotex and computer systems. The list is endless.

Why the resistance? Simply because innovations tend to change, even disrupt, established routines. Resistance to change is a normal human response, and it is inevitable. Not only do potential users resist change, but so do potential manufacturers of the innovation, thus making successful adoption even more difficult.

Here, then, is the dilemma. Innovations are essential for progress. But progress in the long run is feasible only with the change that is inherent in the innovations. The change created by innovations in turn generates barriers of resistance from both manufacturing corporations and potential customers. These resistance barriers can impede, stifle, or even destroy the innovation. What is the solution? Should we be philosophical and resign ourselves to the slow and uncertain path of progress? We think there is a better response.

In this book, we have identified the key corporate and customer barriers that have, time and again, blocked the route to successful innovation. We have suggested strategies to break these barriers and lead the innovation onward to success. We believe every corporation can bring fruitful innovations to market by paying heed to these barriers and then taking direct action to thwart them.

Innovations begin as ideas, but they only bear fruit when finally accepted in the everyday world. It is time we concentrate on mastering that final step into the marketplace.

• • •

Several people have helped us bring our book to market. We would like to acknowledge the patience and persistence of John Mahaney, our editor at John Wiley & Sons. Production of the book would not have been possible without the creative efforts of Barbara Meihoefer's staff at Publication Services, Inc., in

Preface

Champaign, Illinois. In particular, we appreciate the work of Glenn Morrison, Laura Morrison, and Gail Hapke. Finally, our thanks go to the many others, both in Los Angeles and Tucson, who have helped move the book to completion.

JAGDISH N. SHETH
S. RAM

Los Angeles, California
Tucson, Arizona
September 1987

Contents

PART 1 ENCOUNTERING THE BARRIERS	**1**
1. The Need to Innovate	3
2. Corporate Barriers to Innovation	29
3. Customer Barriers to Innovation	63
4. Measuring the Barriers	97
PART 2 BREAKING THE BARRIERS	**139**
5. The Slow and Steady Strategy	141
6. The Grab and Grow Strategy	165
7. The Pick and Protect Strategy	183

8. The Migrate and Maintain Strategy	199
9. Putting It All Together	217
Index	237

Bringing Innovation to Market

Part 1
Encountering the Barriers

Innovation has always been necessary for economic growth and social development. Today, major demographic shifts are putting even greater pressure on business to innovate—to adapt or die. Unfortunately, while the urge to innovate is strong, the structural impediments to the changes innovation brings are also formidable. As a result, vital new products and services never achieve the general acceptance they should, and all of us are the losers.

Successfully bringing innovations to market entails, first, understanding the corporate and customer resistance to innovation and, second, overcoming those barriers. Strategies for accomplishing the latter goal must wait for Part 2 of this book. In Part 1, we will concentrate on defining the problems.

Chapter 1 examines the four basic forces that make the need for innovation so compelling: changing customers, technological breakthroughs, new competition, and changing regulation.

Chapter 2 describes the barriers to innovation that are inherent in the corporate structure, illustrates with real world cases, and offers general solutions.

Chapter 3 performs the same analysis on customer barriers to innovation. It looks at the practical and the psychological factors that cause people to resist even beneficial changes.

Chapter 4 demonstrates how to measure both sets of barriers, because locating and quantifying resistance is the first step in formulating a strategy to overcome it. The chapter focuses on innovations in telecommunications.

1
The Need to Innovate

The most important function of innovation is creating value for the customer by improving the performance–price index of existing products or services. An innovation must offer additional functions or features at the same price, or the same features and functions at a lower price. Reluctance to focus on improving the performance–price index is likely to make even the best U.S. corporations vulnerable. Even IBM.

IBM resisted replacing their 360/370 line of mainframe computers for a long time because customers, who had invested millions of dollars in software and operating systems, would strongly object to spending more for a new generation of machines that did the same job. IBM's competitors, however, took advantage of the company's reluctance to innovate and flooded the market with lower priced machines that would run on IBM operating systems.

Realizing that they were losing their market share, IBM introduced the 4300 series, after nearly a decade of development, in two models: the IBM 4331 and the IBM 4341. The 4331 was the smaller of the two and performed as well as the IBM 370 (model 138); yet it was priced at an incredibly low $65,000, compared to the list price of nearly $350,000 for the old 370 model! The 4341 was bigger and priced at $245,000, about a sixth of the price of the older 370 model.

Simultaneously, IBM also slashed the price of disk memories and peripheral gear. Against an earlier price of $75,000 per megabyte of memory, the price for IBM 4300 memory was set at $15,000, one-fifth of what it had been! In a single move, IBM had increased the performance–price index of its product line sevenfold!

How was this possible? IBM had unerringly zeroed in on new technological developments. They discovered a cheaper method of making logic chips for the new model; each chip could hold up to 704 circuits, compared to only 44 circuits per chip of the most advanced IBM 370 model. The cheaper method of mounting chips on printed circuit boards allowed the IBM 4331 processor to be built with just four and a half circuits (C41/2) boards as against 15 boards required by a comparable older IBM 370 model. IBM also discovered a faster method to manufacture and test the logic chips designed for their 4300 series.

But the greatest competitive advantage IBM gained over the competition came from a new 64,000-bit chip that had 32 times the memory of the standard chips used in the older IBM 370 models. The IBM 4331 was also the first IBM computer that could be used anywhere, not necessarily in the main computer room. It did not require air-conditioning, and it was flexible enough to be connected to other computers. Needless to say, within days of announcing the 4300 series, IBM had orders booked for three years ahead. It was clearly a case of a corporate giant recovering lost ground after belatedly realizing that innovation is the best weapon to improve performance–price value for the customer.

IBM's experience indicates that an established company that recognizes a need to innovate can innovate effectively. IBM is, of course, not alone in their assessment of the need. A recent

The Need to Innovate

survey conducted by Booz, Allen & Hamilton, the consulting firm, indicated that business executives in all sectors of the U.S. economy believe that innovation will be the prime ingredient of industry profits and growth in the coming decades.

In fact, the survey indicated that most executives believe new products and services created through innovation drive, skunk works, and intrapreneuring will generate one-third of the business growth and 40 percent of the business profits in the near future. This is both a remarkable expectation for business and a difficult challenge for management, considering that the mature U.S. economy is bottom heavy with a very large base of existing technologies, products, and services.

Innovation takes on even greater significance in the services sector as the United States shifts from an industrial to a postindustrial society. Major societal changes always place a premium on adaptability. Innovation will be the key success factor as well for such less-developed nations as China, Brazil, and India as they strive to move their economies into the industrial age. Innovation was the hallmark of U.S. growth when the economy began the shift from an agricultural to an industrial society in the late nineteenth to early twentieth century. Innovation has always been a corporate and national obsession. Today's competitive conditions justify that fascination.

Our book is not, however, about innovation as such. Instead, our purpose is to explain why corporations and customers actually resist innovation even though they see that it is both necessary and desirable. We intend to identify corporation- and customer-erected barriers that thwart the innovative process. We will also assess strategies for breaking through those barriers.

We believe the concepts developed in this book are equally applicable to the industrial, consumer, and service sectors. We hope the real world examples and case histories will demonstrate their universal business application. First, however, we want to examine specific reasons why the economic environment demands consistent innovative activity.

Four distinct forces are chiefly responsible for the increasing

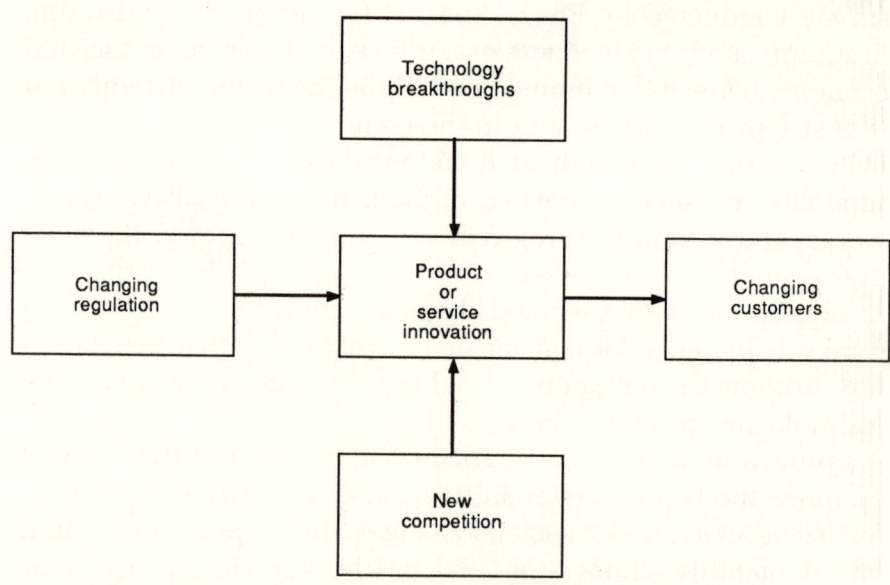

Figure 1.1 Forces responsible for business innovation

importance of product and service innovation in the the 1980s and beyond (see Figure 1.1). Innovation is the only possible response to technological breakthroughs and the changing character of competition, regulation, and customers themselves.

CHANGING CUSTOMERS

According to Peter Drucker, the purpose of business is to create and retain customers. Unfortunately, most businesses focus too much on creating new customers and not enough on retaining the existing customer base. Consequently, even though certain customers' needs and requirements may change, businesses tend to keep their products and services the same. The result is a widening gap between product/service benefits and customer needs, leaving firms competitively vulnerable. Companies can identify innovative products or services that are more in line with changing or emerging market needs by examining the national demographic profile. There are three fundamental demographic trends taking place in the United States right now that are having, and will continue to have, profound effects on business in general. Their impact is felt directly on consumer products and services and indirectly on industrial products and services. These trends are (1) the aging of the U.S. population, (2) the emergence of dual-income families, and (3) the increase in the number of single-person households.

Aging of the Population

Americans are growing old together. The median age of the nation in 1980 was 30 years; by the end of the century it will be almost 40. In short, America will become one decade older in two decades! We are getting older partly because we are living longer, but mostly because we are producing fewer children. In fact, the U.S. Bureau of the Census has estimated that if this trend toward lower fertility and mortality rates continues, the United States will have a negative population base by the year 2040, that is, the population will have actually started to *decline*.

As the population ages, former needs become less important and newer needs begin to surface. The resulting fissure is known as a market gap. Three basic needs are emerging in the United States for which we currently have inadequate or obsolete products and services. Market gaps are opening up in health preservation, wealth preservation, and personal security.

Keeping Healthy. The first major consequence of the aging population is the dramatic rise in health care needs of the society. People are more interested in preserving their health and maintaining their physical fitness. As the bloom of youth fades, we worry more about what we eat, what we drink, and what we breathe both in the office and the home environment.

Consequently, health care products and services will grow

at a faster rate than they ever have. The health care industry will become the leading sector of the U.S. economy. However, the concern for health goes beyond the health care industry. It is, and will continue to be, manifested in the foods people eat, in the beverages they drink, in the clothing they wear, and in the personal care items they consume. Unfortunately, yesterday's products or services, designed primarily for the baby boom generation of the 1950s and 1960s, are either inadequate or inappropriate for the older population. Appliances, automobiles, homes, recreation and leisure products, and indeed offerings for any economic activity must be redesigned for older people with more mature concerns.

WHERE'S THE BEEF? It is a biological fact that as people grow older, they change what they eat and how much they eat. Older people tend to eat less red meat, for example, because they are concerned about animal fat in their diet. This is a growing trend among younger people, too, and is having a significant impact on the beef industry. Not only is the per capita consumption of beef declining, but the distribution channels are shifting from the supermarkets and grocery stores to restaurants and fast-food establishments. This is because middle-aged and older people tend to have fewer children at home. Therefore, they cook less at home and either eat out more frequently or bring home prepared meals from restaurants and fast-food outlets. When they do eat meat, therefore, it tends to be while dining out.

The declining consumption of beef is having a direct impact on the beef industry. The American cowboy is unable to survive economically and is therefore becoming a vanishing breed as more and more ranchers get out of the cattle business. Similarly, the meat packing business is consolidating because smaller firms cannot survive a declining demand. Both cattle ranching and meat packing are winding up in the hands of fewer but bigger business units. The survivors must innovate because their customers are no longer traditional supermarkets, but restaurants and fast-food chains. Specifically, they must modify their physical distribution systems and become more demand-driven, since neither restaurants nor fast-food outlets carry large freezers or have the storage capacity to buy the meat ahead of time.

Indirectly, the beef industry must encourage both the cattle feed and the biogenetic industries to innovate and help produce better beef that is more suitable for older people's needs. Furthermore, it must do so without raising the price. Otherwise, consumers will shift their demand to chicken, fish, and fresh fruits and vegetables. In short, the beef industry must *create value* by increasing the performance–price ratio through innovation in biogenetics and animal feed technologies.

CAFFEINE-FREE. People also change their drinking habits as they grow older. This is perhaps best illustrated by the coffee industry. As people grow older, their tolerance for caffeine goes down. The coffee industry has responded well by offering a variety of decaffeinated coffees. The new products, however, require a significant shift in coffee processing technologies. This change has an indirect impact on machinery, coffee beans, and the blending processes. We should not be surprised if coffee growing nations such as Brazil begin investing in significant plant genetics research so that they can grow low caffeine beans to start with.

It is also amusing to note that there seems to be no direct market for the caffeine taken out in the processing of decaffeinated coffees. Traditionally, coffee makers such as General Foods sold the extracted caffeine to soft drink makers, such as Coca Cola. But these manufacturers do not want caffeine either because their customers—the baby boomers—are now much older and want less caffeine in *their* soft drinks. The coffee makers must innovate to find new and different applications for caffeine as a byproduct. Who knows? There may be some use for caffeine in industrial applications.

Finally, as the population grows older and the nation's food preparation and food consumption habits change, the appliance industry will also be affected. The family-sized dishwasher, which was popular in the 1960s, is already too big for the empty nesters. A need for a compact dishwasher, a compact refrigerator, and a compact oven is beginning to emerge. As people buy compact appliances, the parts manufacturers; assembly machinery manufacturers; and shipping, trucking, and packaging businesses are all indirectly affected.

In short, the changing demographic pattern has both a direct impact on the consumer product or service and an indirect impact on all those businesses that depend on that consumer product or service for their derived demand.

Staying Wealthy. A second major concern of the older consumer is the preservation of wealth he or (increasingly) she has accumulated over a period of two or more decades of full-time work. Most estimates are that the net worth of an average household today exceeds $150,000 (including pension(s), insurance, home equity, and personal property), which is at least six times greater than the average annual income.

The U.S. economy is now less driven by traditional Keynesian economics. Keynes' theory of consumer demand holds that people's desire to spend or save depends on their *income* levels. Therefore, the government can influence demand, inflation, and employment if it can regulate people's income by tax laws and monetary policies such as interest rates. His theory is currently very popular among many developing nations, just as it was in the United States in the 1930s and 1940s, when people had limited savings and primarily depended on their weekly or monthly paycheck.

However, these conditions no longer characterize U.S. society. Since World War II, the average American family has accumulated a significant amount of wealth in the form of home equity, pension money, life insurance, and inheritances. Thus, the theories of economist Milton Friedman are more relevant today. Friedman believes that sources of *permanent income or wealth* can generate their own income, which must then be examined to determine their influence on people's desire to save or to spend. A recent survey printed in *USA Today* reported that more than 11 percent of the people with annual incomes of $240,000 were unemployed. Their wealth was generating wealth.

Consequently, the financial services industry needs to innovate products and services that are focused more on wealth and less on the monthly paycheck. This checking account mentality of most institutions must give way to financial planning and portfolio management. Today, the average consumer is more interested in refinancing or borrowing against equity than in obtaining a first-time mortgage. People are more interested in estate planning, in raising capital to start a business, and in investing in the stock market or even riskier ventures.

This need for individual wealth preservation has a national or macro aspect as well. It has an indirect impact on corporate pension plans, on the social security system, on the stock market, and even more fundamentally on the tax policy of state and federal governments.

For example, many employees are now willing to retire early from their regular jobs because the significant amount of savings accumulated in corporate pension funds can be easily utilized for starting a business venture or for investing in higher-yielding investments. Therefore, corporations are under a lot of pressure to repay the pension money to their employees. This creates an adverse impact on the availability of very cheap, or free, capital.

Similarly, because people are willing to take more risks as their wealth increases, the stock market can no longer afford to ignore average citizens as investors today because such citizens represent billions of dollars of potential capital infusion.

Finally, the tax policy of the country must focus on people's desire to preserve and leverage their wealth. Policy must, therefore, shift focus away from employment-based income to include investment-related income, as the latter becomes a more significant part of people's total assets. Also, consumption and wealth taxes become more meaningful ways of generating revenues than the traditional income taxes.

Keeping Safe. When a nation grows older, a third major basic need emerges: the safety and security of persons and property. When people get older, they feel more vulnerable, and at the same time they believe they are less able to protect themselves from physical harm. Security systems and personal weapons for self-protection become more attractive. Older people are more open as well to appeals for law and order and public safety. These needs are not currently being addressed in any creative or innovative manner. A market gap exists that can be filled.

Dual-Income Families

A second demographic shift—even more dramatic in its impact on existing technologies, products, and services—is the increasing prevalence of households in which both husband and wife work outside the home in income producing occupations. Today more than 55 percent of all women have a job or career away from the home. This figure will rise to at least 65 percent by the year 2000. Indeed, in many large metropolitan areas such as New York, Boston, and Los Angeles, dual incomes have become necessary to maintain the family or the household. In other words, a household with two working spouses is no longer a matter of choice, as it was in the 1950s and 1960s.

Time Is More Than Money. When both spouses work outside the home, both time and money resources must be redistributed. For example, as much as 55 to 60 hours of the week must now be spent in work related activities—preparing for work, traveling to work, and actually working—instead of caring for the home, raising children, or shopping. This shift creates several immediate consequences. First, discretionary time to purchase and consume products and services is now available only during

Changing Customers

evenings and weekends, thus requiring changes in the opening and closing hours in all retailing situations, from grocery and department stores to professional and financial services.

Traditional business hours are in direct conflict with purchasing hours, creating a market gap in time and place between suppliers and consumers. Significant innovation is needed in warehousing, physical distribution, delivery, selling, and customer service. Indeed, it is not enough to promise that your service person will come on a given day; it will become necessary to pinpoint within the hour when he or she will visit the home.

A second consequence of time redistribution is that many home activities performed by the homemaker are becoming commercial opportunities or major markets. More homemakers are delegating child care, cooking, and cleaning to outside vendors. Eating out has become more common. Even meals eaten at home are frequently prepared by someone else as we turn to frozen dinners and take-out from restaurants to save time. Indeed, the kitchen has become much less a place for food preparation and much more a place for food consumption.

Third, we are becoming a time-poor society. Time, especially nonbudgeted or discretionary time, is becoming more scarce. People are seeking innovative ways to save time and innovative products and services to minimize wasted time. Time management books, programs, and products are popular. Waiting in line is less easily tolerated; waiting rooms are aggressively resented; *waiting* has itself become a dirty word. People want instant procurement, instant information, and instant gratification. All of this is generating enormous market gaps in those highly procedural service industries—hotels, airlines, restaurants, and hospitals—that require a lot of paperwork and record-keeping and are therefore susceptible to long time delays while serving customers.

Where the Money Goes. The dual-income household has a second major impact. It is redistributing incomes within the society. In the 1950s and the 1960s, when the one-wage-earner household was in the majority, a large middle-class mass market dominated the nation. Today, the middle class is on the decline. It is rapidly becoming supplemented by a larger affluent class and a larger low-income class. The bulge in the middle of the income distribution curve is being pushed to the ends. As a result, there are three distinct market segments: premium (affluent), best value (middle class), and affordable (new poor) products and services in virtually every sector of the economy.

In the process, companies that dominated the middle-class mass markets with midrange prices are struggling to survive. But at the same time, premium products and services are experiencing a spectacular rise in demand. Witness the growth of gourmet foods, luxury cars, premium appliances, designer clothing, and premium retail services. Also, the new poor are trying to economize by patronizing offshore brand names and wholesale warehouses.

The income redistribution of households strongly suggests a fundamental change. It means that markets are becoming divergent and, therefore, no single product or service at one price point can satisfy a majority of the customers in the marketplace.

Emergence of Single-Person Households

A third demographic change in the U.S. economy is the spectacular rise of single-person households. Such households currently represent nearly 25 percent of the total and should rise even more by the year 2000 as the aging population begins to live alone. Simultaneously, more young people are voluntarily choosing to live alone rather than start a family. In fact, the traditional family, consisting of the breadwinner, the homemaker, and the children, now comprises only 7 percent of all U.S. households.

One Is a Lonely Number. The single life-style, whether assumed by choice or by necessity, creates distinctive needs. One such

Changing Customers 15

need is combatting loneliness. A number of products and services, ranging from singles bars and physical fitness centers to Club Med, have become more popular as a consequence of society's loneliness. This phenomenon has received a lot of attention. Less well recognized are the products and services designed to provide an escape from loneliness. These include drugs, meditation, and radio talk shows.

Adult Living Is In. Another major consequence of living alone is the growing prevalence of adult-oriented life-styles. Products and services designed for the family are less appropriate for this segment of the population. Large refrigerators, station wagons, and retail outlets such as Sears and J.C. Penney do not fit single adults. A number of television shows—Bill Cosby's aside—do, however, reflect the trend. Gone are the days of such family programs as *The Ed Sullivan Show*, *Ozzie and Harriet*, and *The Red Skelton Show*. Today's most popular programs include *Sixty Minutes*, *Dallas*, and *Miami Vice*, which are all adult-oriented programs. The same phenomenon is evident on radio and cable television programming and in newspapers and magazines.

The Focus Is on the Individual. Finally, a third major consequence of living alone is the emergence of individualistic life-styles. People who do not share with others create a different unit of consumption. Products and services designed for a family of four are obsolete. Instead, products and services need to be redesigned for per capita consumption. This shift applies to such basic necessities as food, shelter, insurance, health care, automobiles, and appliances, as well as to discretionary recreation and other leisure activities.

The food companies will be forced to offer individual servings (soup for one). The homes of the future will be much smaller than the traditional three-bedroom, 1600 square foot home. Employee benefits such as group insurance plans must be offered on an individual rather than a family basis. Similarly, the automobile must be redesigned so that it becomes a personal car rather than the old family station wagon. Appliances, as we have already noted, will become more compact. Finally, recreation and leisure activities must be redesigned so that a single person can enjoy them. Team sports will give way to personal sports; family magazines will give way to specialty or life-style magazines; group tours will give way to individual travel (i.e., no more double occupancy rates in group tours); and so on.

The changing demographics of the 1970s and 1980s, as described, will have a more dramatic and longer lasting impact on the economic structure of the United States than the baby boom of the 1940s and 1950s. The aging population and the increase in both dual-income families and single-person households will generate a gap between the products and services based on the present technologies, on the one hand, and customer needs, wants, and life-styles, on the other. Innovation, especially through technological breakthroughs, offers the chance to bridge that gap and should thus be a major strategic objective for the corporation.

TECHNOLOGICAL BREAKTHROUGHS

Necessity is the mother of invention, so the saying goes. Changing customer needs have created market gaps and therefore a lot of necessity. Fortunately, they have also provided plenty of opportunities to entrepreneurs, big and small, to take advantage of technological progress. The last 200 years of invention are instructive.

The history of technology is both fascinating and dramatic. Since the Industrial Revolution, we have witnessed several technological ages, each one more dramatic in its impact on business and society. To fully appreciate how technological breakthroughs affect business in particular and society in general, it is necessary to examine the roles technology plays.

Technological Breakthroughs

Technology performs two fundamental functions. First, it increases the *efficiency* of natural and artificial resources. Efficiency is achieved when resources are able to perform economic tasks faster and to their fullest capacity. This process is commonly referred to as the economy of scale or the learning curve. Second, technology also increases the *versatility* of resources by enabling them to perform tasks differently or in different settings. In other words, technology enables a resource to perform unrelated tasks in different situations. It allows the user to become a generalist rather than remain a specialist. This phenomenon is commonly called the economy of scope.

The greater the efficiency and versatility of resources created by a technological breakthrough, the greater its impact on society and business. Unfortunately, it is often difficult to predict or anticipate whether a new technological breakthrough will result in higher efficiency and/or versatility. However, it has been easy in retrospect to recognize and even measure each major technology's impact on society. For example, while we did not fully appreciate the total impact of the automobile or the telephone or electricity when they first appeared, we can now see how much they have altered the way we live.

The Ages of Technology

When we take the long view of the various technological ages, the effects of technology are clearer still. The industrial revolution started the *mechanical age* based on the discoveries and exploitation of scientific concepts of mechanics and physics. It dramatically increased the productivity and efficiency of the agricultural sector. Industrialization divorced production from consumption in physical distance and in time by facilitating faster transportation, better storage, and mass production. Factories and railways are the obvious symbols of the industrial society.

The mechanical age was soon displaced by the *electromechanical age*, with the discovery of electricity. It not only dramatically increased the productivity of manufacturing, transportation, and storage, but it added significant versatility to economic activities. Electricity narrowed the economic gap between urban and rural markets. It broadened the geographical scope of markets that could be reached and served. Telephones, radios, automobiles, and appliances are the symbols of this age.

The electromechanical age was supplemented by the *chemical age*, with major technical breakthroughs in biology and chemistry. The chemical age increased the productivity of the industrial society by successfully substituting manmade substances for natural resources—drugs, nutritional supplements, artificial flavors and colors, fertilizers, herbicides, insecticides, detergents, and so on—and thereby removing resource bottlenecks. It speeded up the process of growth and development in plants, animals, and even human beings through agricultural, pharmaceutical, and industrial chemicals. The chemical age expanded the economy by making materials and products both affordable and available.

Today, we are witnessing similar technological breakthroughs as we shift from the chemical to the *biogenetic age* and from the electromechanical to the *electronic age*. Both ages are adding enormous versatility to resources, in addition to improving their efficiency. In that respect, the impact of these two technological bases may be unparalleled.

The fundamental breakthrough of the electronics age is generally considered to be the development of (1) the transistor, then (2) the printed circuit, and finally (3) the microchip. Microchip semiconductors are now regarded as a national strategic resource for technological and industrial development, and are comparable to minerals and oil.

Semiconductors have dramatically increased the efficiency and versatility of resources through their innovative application in electronic computers and electronic communications. These advances enable us to process and distribute information on a real time basis across vast geographical distances. For example, who would have imagined at the time of the Crusades that Christian churches today would be able to broadcast services all over the globe with the use of satellites? Better yet, who would have dreamt only a few years ago that local priests and ministers would be able to store and process information about church attendance and charitable contributions and plan their weekly religious services with the aid of personal computers?

Similar contributions are made by the laser. The versatility of laser technology is truly impressive. It is the basis for such diverse innovations as microsurgery techniques, fatigue detection devices, garment cutting machinery, fiberoptics, and Star Wars defense weapons.

Finally, the biogenetic experiments that led to the understanding of the DNA structure are today generating such innovations as the superseed, with its own stored pesticide; improved fertilizers and herbicides; and genetically bred cows with greater milk-producing capacity. Biogenetic advances are also creating a race of bigger, heartier, tastier superchickens and are controlling genetic defects in both plants and animals.

In summary, the basic technological advances have enabled businesses to innovate new products and services that are both superior in performance and cheaper in cost than existing alternatives. In fact, 9 out of 10 executives surveyed by Booz, Allen & Hamilton cited technological advancements as the primary source of innovations in corporations.

NEW COMPETITION

After more than half a century of industrialization on a global basis, it seems that most sectors of the world economy, including agriculture, manufacturing, and retail services, are at the maturity stage of their industry life cycle. Mature industries tend toward consolidation, with a handful of big players dominating. We see this pattern in the automobile and the appliance industries. It is also prevalent in the food industry as well as in most types of retailing. Consolidation is certainly the rule in such basic industries as steel, aluminum, machine tools, industrial chemicals, and pharmaceuticals. It is also true of most phases of agribusiness.

The oligopolistic nature of industry evolution results in strong price and/or promotion competition among the big players, and each has the staying power to put up a good fight in the market share battle. This intense price/promotion competition increases the cost and decreases the price, resulting in a profit squeeze. Companies, therefore, seek an alternate approach to price/promotion competition. Most pin their hopes on innovation, because they believe that successful innovation will (1) expand the market, (2) motivate the customer to pay higher prices, or (3) at least reduce the costs.

The innovative process does have a record of success. For example, microprocessors have expanded the computer market from big business to small business; we are paying higher prices for more convenient services and products in general; and the sharp experience curves associated with the semiconductor industry have reduced the cost of manufacturing in most industries.

Three new competitive dimensions seem to drive corporate innovation: global competition, productivity, and quality assurance.

Global Competition

Virtually everyone agrees that competition is becoming global. In other words, it is inevitable that domestic U.S. manufacturers and marketers will have to expand their market boundaries to other parts of the world as foreign competitors, especially from Japan and Korea, expand their market boundaries into the United States. Some experts even suggest that it is necessary to be strong in all three major markets—North America, Europe, and Japan—to successfully compete in the world market.

A number of factors have contributed to the emergence of global competition. First, since World War II the General Agreements on Trade and Tariffs (GATT) and other economic alliances such as the European Common Market have reduced trade barriers and tariffs, thus allowing products and services from offshore to enter domestic markets. Second, we have also witnessed a significant transfer of technology from the advanced to the developing nations, especially in such basic industries as steel, chemicals, transportation, and agriculture. Technology transfer still continues, but with some variations. It is, for instance, more prevalent in the high-tech areas of computers, telecommunications, and biogenetics. At the same time, there is a reverse transfer of technology from recently developed nations such as Brazil, India, and Korea in the low-tech industries of components, raw materials, and labor-intensive services. However you measure it, we seem to have a strong coexistence of technology transfer and international trade.

A third reason for the increasing global competition is of more recent vintage. For the first time, we are witnessing global mergers, acquisitions, and strategic alliances. For example, virtually all U.S. automobile companies have strategic alliances with their competitors in Japan and Europe. General Motors has aligned with Toyota, Ford partially owns Mazda, and Chrysler has a significant ownership of Mitsubishi. Similar trends are found in the consumer electronics industry, in pharmaceuticals, and in retailing. This trend toward global mergers, acquisitions, and strategic alliances is likely to spread into other industries, such as appliances, textiles, professional services (advertising, consulting, auditing), and even microprocessors and biogenetics.

One major consequence of global competition is product innovation. In most instances, it becomes necessary to modify the product or service to accommodate local regulations, material scarcities, or climatic differences. For example, foreign cars must modify their bumpers and add a catalytic converter to enter the U.S. market because our product safety and pollution control standards are different. Denmark and many other countries do not permit metal cans; foreign beverage firms must package their beer or soft drinks in bottles. Furthermore, all beer bottles are identical in Denmark, and they are recycled. Therefore, all a company can do is paste on its own label.

The best example of adapting to international differences is the story of selling Chiclet chewing gum in India. First, the high humidity and temperature required individual wrappers. Second, the gum had to be sold in packages containing only two pieces to reduce the purchase price, thus making it more affordable for the average consumer.

Even structural differences may cause adjustments in global markets. Because voltage current and cycles, as well as plug units, are different from country to country, electronics firms must develop more *universal products* (110 or 220 volts, 50 or 60 cycles, plugs for different input jacks) or offer separate customized variations. In short, innovation becomes necessary as market boundaries are expanded by global competition.

Productivity Drive

New competition also focuses on improving the productivity of physical and human resources. As price competition, especially from offshore manufacturers and marketers, has intensified, most U.S. corporations have begun to concentrate on improving the productivity of the worker and the physical facilities. For example, CAD/CAM (computer-aided design and manufacturing), LAN (local area networks), office automation, integrated manufacturing, and integrated information services have been tried and tested as productivity tools. In addition, classical time and motion studies associated with Taylor's scientific management principles are being revitalized to examine the redundancy and incompatibility inherent in the flow of business operations.

The identification of operational problems spurs the desire for innovative solutions. Innovation drives are organized partly to encourage worker participation and motivation and partly to create new solutions. Workers welcome a chance for recognition and involvement, since they are often a neglected source of valuable ideas. In short, one more reason for increasing interest in innovation is the issue of productivity.

Quality Assurance

A third focus of new competition is concern for product/service quality. For the first time, everyone has come to realize that low-price, low-quality products (cheap goods) have a short life cycle. In other words, what the customer wants is not cheap products/services at low prices but good quality products/services at a low price. Japan embraced this truth soon after World War II and instituted strong quality assurance programs *across the board* as a national drive. The high-quality products manufactured in Japan, combined with strong export incentives from the government, resulted in the best value offering in the world markets.

The dominance of Japan as a major economic power in less than a quarter of a century has made both the United States and the European manufacturers realize that low prices alone do not sell products. Today, therefore, there is strong interest in such quality assurance programs as quality circles, worker training, and factory automation to improve the real value of products or services. This trend is dramatically demonstrated in the automobile industry, which has recently made a turnaround from cheap goods (low-price, low-quality) to best-value (low-price, high-quality) products.

One consequence of quality assurance programs has been innovation, whether it is in work flow, in material substitution, or in manufacturing processes. Work flow is now, for instance, based on the just-in-time concept, which reverses the traditional process. Rather than moving forward from raw materials to components to assembly, now the work flows from assembly to components to raw materials. In other words, the assembly of the finished product determines *when* to produce components, and the component manufacturers determine when to buy raw materials. A great deal of material substitution has taken place in the field of consumer electronics. Plastics have replaced wood and metal; wires and tubes are now all solid state. The manufacturing process is also becoming increasingly computerized. What is called process control is basically factory automation. Rather than having separate supervisors at each stage of the process, one computer monitors, coordinates, and controls the total flow of activities.

CHANGING REGULATION

Breaking up Is Big Business

Rapidly changing regulations also encourage product/service innovation. There are three specific regulatory areas of greatest significance. The first is a worldwide trend toward deregulation or privatization of regulated monopolies, such as those in telecommunications, the airlines, banking, insurance, health care, and other professional services. The most common rationale is that regulated industries tend to be less efficient and discourage innovation. The argument goes that competition and/or privatization will generate both operational efficiency and market effectiveness through a massive restructuring of the industry as well as by an internal reorganization of the regulated monopolies.

The airline industry is a dramatic case study. Since deregulation in 1978, cost efficiency as well as product differentiation have become corporate watchwords. Two-tier wage structures and tough bargaining with the unions are commonplace. A greater number of airlines after the same markets means greater efforts by each to differentiate themselves from the competition. The result is a proliferation of innovative services: computerized reservations and tickets, special meals, variety in refreshments, stereo music, movies, more carry-on luggage, and so on.

A similar pattern is occurring in the telecommunications industry. Not long ago, the telephone industry offered only the basic black telephone and dial tone services (plain old telephone service—the famous POTS). Today, however, customers can choose from a significant variety of telephone terminals as well as telephone services both for local and long distance calls (see chapter 4). In short, deregulation of industry or privatization of the regulated monopoly generates a need for true innovation.

Standards for Order

A second area of changing regulation involves setting new technical standards. New standards are created for two reasons. First, a deregulated industry still requires some sort of regulatory body to set technical standards to ensure compatibility and comparability of products and services. Second, when the distinctions between products and services become blurred by technological evolution, the regulatory agencies need to set new standards to redefine the market boundaries.

The telecommunications industry has seen both of these forces come into play. Virtually every regulatory agency is setting up technical standards for the interface between the telephone networks and the telephone terminals as the latter business is deregulated. Similarly, as we evolve toward information age technologies, the boundaries between communications and computers are getting blurred, thus requiring the regulatory agencies to set standards, even in the international area where the Integrated Services Defined Network (ISDN) is now in force. The new technical standards often result in innovation by redefining the capability of the telecommunications industry. Rather than limit the use of telephone lines for conversation (voice) medium, ISDN technical standards allow people to communicate with equal efficiency through voice, data, picture, and text media. The changing regulations encourage switch manufacturers, terminal manufacturers, as well as transmission manufacturers to innovate at considerably more sophisticated levels of technology.

Standards for Safety

A third area of changing regulation that demands innovation is the creation of tougher product/service safety standards. Most governments, especially in advanced countries, have become increasingly concerned with either the main effects or the side effects of the use or misuse of some products. And many governments have taken action. Virtually all sectors of the economy are affected by tougher product/service safety standards.

For example, in agricultural and industrial chemicals, firms must create substitutes for banned substances such as DDT and asbestos. In the processed food industry, companies must work around labeling requirements and restrictions on the use of certain artificial flavors and colors. The automobile industry has had to meet new safety and mileage standards. Finally, we see safety standards being put in place for such universal services as security, health care, and financial services. And the trend is likely to grow stronger.

RESISTANCE TO INNOVATION

Ironically, as the demand for innovation increases so does the resistance. Corporations resist even though innovation often means survival. Customers resist innovation even though it means better products and services.

The purpose of this book is to explain why. If we understand why innovations are resisted, we might be able to design strategies to overcome the resistance. We have found that the problem is not, surprisingly, an intense aversion to change. The cause is structural. Corporations and customers experience barriers that paralyze the desire to innovate. The more radical the innovation,

Resistance to Innovation

the greater the structural barriers and, therefore, the greater the resistance. The solution is to understand the impact an innovation will have on the existing corporate and customer structural dimensions and then creatively channel the innovative drive either around or through the structural impediment.

It is our contention that we do *not* have a cultural problem. Both corporate managers and consumers, especially in industrialized countries, are culturally pro-innovation. They believe that technology, if properly harnessed, is good for mankind. The resistance to innovate, we repeat, comes from structural elements.

Corporate resistance arises from the structural barriers inherent in expertise, operations, resources, regulation, and market access. Customer resistance is built with the structural barriers inherent in usage, value, risk, tradition, and image. The remainder of the book is dedicated to describing those barriers and defining strategies to overcome them.

Chapter 2 is devoted to corporate barriers. Each barrier is illustrated with real world examples from different sectors of the economy. We also provide solutions to the problems each barrier creates.

Chapter 3 is devoted to customer barriers. Each barrier is discussed with examples from various sectors of the economy: consumer durables, nondurables, services, industrial supplies, and capital goods. Again, we provide solutions to each barrier problem.

Chapter 4 shows how to measure the five corporate and five customer barriers. In order to demonstrate how each industry is likely to contain innovations that will face different degrees and combinations of structural corporate and customer resistance, we have selected the telecommunications industry to illustrate the possible variations. We will evaluate eight different innovations in that industry on all 10 dimensions of corporate and customer resistance. The innovations include videotex, ISDN, digital services, cellular mobile telephones, electronic mail, lifeline services, the toll-free number service, and custom calling services.

Part 2 of the book examines various strategies for introducing innovations in the marketplace. Chapter 5 discusses the Slow and Steady Strategy, which is most appropriate when both the corporate and the customer structural barriers are significant.

Chapter 6 discusses the Grab and Grow Strategy, which is best suited when neither the corporate nor the customer barriers are significant impediments to innovation.

Chapter 7 is devoted to describing the Pick and Protect Strategy, which is very appropriate when customer barriers are significant and difficult, but corporate barriers are easy to resolve.

Finally, chapter 8 discusses the Migrate and Maintain Strategy, which is very useful when corporate barriers are difficult to overcome, but customer barriers are nonsignificant or can be easily hurdled.

Chapter 9 puts all the concepts together in an integrated framework for easier implementation. Our goals are first to promote understanding of the phenomenon of innovation resistance and then to offer practical solutions. Necessary innovation is too often thwarted by structural barriers. An informed corporation has the power to focus its resources and break through the barriers to a brighter future.

Steele, L. "Managers' Misconceptions About Technology." *Harvard Business Review*, Nov-Dec. 1983, 133–140.

Uttal, B. "How the 4300 fits IBM's New Strategy." *Fortune*, July 30, 1979, 58–62.

Booz, Allen & Hamilton Inc. "New Product Management For the 1980s." Chicago, 1982.

"New Growth Industires." *Business Week*. Sept. 3, 1979, 100.

2
Corporate Barriers to Innovation

In an effort to capitalize on the new satellite technology available for television programming, United Satellite Communications, Inc. (USCI) was established in 1983. Its major objective was to introduce a direct-broadcast-by-satellite (DBS) service that would bring programs like those on cable television to areas where cable was not available, and possibly even compete with cable television elsewhere. USCI leased five transponders on a Canadian satellite for $1 million a month. They recruited General Instrument to provide $9 million as up-front investment and to produce the 3- to 4-foot (diameter) dishes and other hardware needed to pick up the satellite's signal. USCI persuaded Prudential Insurance to invest nearly $45 million. They purchased movies, sports programs, and television reruns to support five of their eight channels.

In late 1983, USCI began offering service to customers in Indianapolis at a one-time charge of $300 to install and wire the satellite dish and $49.95 per month for service, including maintenance and equipment rental. But the response from the Indianapolis market was unenthusiastic. USCI then moved into

Chicago and Washington, D.C. in early 1984, but subscribers numbered only about 1000. Since the DBS market for U.S. households without cable was estimated at 7,000,000, it was clear that USCI had not made inroads into the market.

This setback particularly distressed management at USCI, since they had expected to reap the benefits of early entry into the field. What caused the disappointing results? First, the customers were quite simply unwilling to accept the product. Not only did the choice of programs and the price of the system fail to meet their expectations, but their needs were already adequately satisfied by existing alternatives. Additionally, USCI found it difficult to reach the customers who *were* interested. The installation of satellite dishes is not an easy job: A two-man crew takes nearly half a day to install each dish, and each installation costs anywhere from $140 to $240. This difficulty slowed the pace of market penetration considerably and forced USCI to seek outside distribution channels, such as Radio Shack, which had a large installation force in the field, to meet even the limited demand.

Management at USCI thought they had all the advantages—sound financial backing, technical expertise, early entry into a promising field—and yet their venture met with one disappointment after another. And their story is not unique. Many managers who, like those at USCI, are thoroughly convinced that corporate growth and survival depend on successful innovation, but they have nonetheless encountered unexpected barriers that have, for them, proved insurmountable. It is our fundamental belief that such failures result, not from some deficiency in corporate culture, but from a *structural* dysfunction within the organization. Most managers are pro-innovation in their values, perceptions, and attitudes; it is in the process of implementing these values, perceptions, and attitudes that a kind of paralysis seems to set in—and for clearly definable reasons.

We have identified five major barriers to innovation that are inherent in the structure of many corporations and that must be clearly understood by top management before any innovation drive can hope to succeed. These include barriers of expertise, operations, resources, regulation, and market access. The expertise and operations barriers are both problems of specialization, in technology and organization, respectively. They involve the inability of many corporations to integrate new patterns of behavior into rigidly established routines. The resource, regulation, and market access barriers are problems of environment. They refer, respectively, to the inability to acquire necessary capital, the inability to overcome regulatory hurdles, and the inability to reach prospective consumers in an efficient and effective manner.

In this chapter, we will define all five barriers in detail, provide examples from industry, and offer several practical strategies for overcoming them. There is no question that innovation is a very difficult task, but the first step in planning any successful campaign is understanding the enemy, and these five inherent structural corporate barriers are truly enemies within the camp of any innovative organization. Here you will learn to recognize them—and to surmount them.

THE SPECIALIZATION TRAP

As surprising as it may sound, the more highly specialized an organization, the less likely it is to make successful innovations. This is because as the technology and organization of a company become increasingly focused and complex, the patterns of corporate behavior to increase efficiency, reduce cost, and avoid error become more and more rigidly established. And rigidly established patterns are difficult to break, whether they are patterns of research and development or manufacture and assembly. This tendency of specialization to lead to rigidity is the cause of two closely related corporate barriers to innovation: the expertise barrier and the operations barrier. We will deal with each separately.

The Expertise Barrier

In a time when the technological sophistication of even the most common products and services is increasing at a mind-boggling rate, one would expect technological specialization to be the key to successful innovation. In fact, just the reverse is true. With the exception of such national treasures as Bell Laboratories and Arthur D. Little, most organizations tend to have not only a high degree of technical specialization but also a concomitantly low degree of technical versatility. Take the giants of the pharmaceutical industry, for example: As a direct result of their highly specialized technologies, most have only a few major innovations to their credit. Often their entire revenue depends on one or two patented drugs such as Darvon, Tagamet, or Aspartame. Their specialized knowledge is simply not versatile enough to transfer to another, related product line. Similarly, the specialized expertise of the steel industry cannot be transferred to the manufacture of aluminum or plastics, which are often the direct substitutes of steel. When such companies do attempt to move out of their immediate area of specialization, they are rarely successful. IBM failed in the duplicating machine business; Xerox failed in computers. It has even proven difficult for coffee companies to succeed in tea.

These companies are all victims, as well as beneficiaries, of the experience curve, which is the tendency of companies with a high degree of specialization to organize for efficiency rather than experimentation. The experience curve encourages depth of knowledge, but sacrifices the breadth of knowledge necessary for successful innovation. It allows companies to make improvements on their established products, to ring changes on them, but not to make entirely new ones—just as a skilled ophthalmologist may find new and better ways of treating glaucoma, but would be hard-pressed to apply that knowledge to the field of cardiac bypass surgery.

The degree of technical specialization and, therefore, the

The Specialization Trap

adverse effects of the expertise barrier are even greater in services than in manufacture. Without acquisitions or mergers, for example, it is almost impossible for an insurance company to compete in banking, brokerage, or even real estate. Not surprisingly, this is also true of the communications industry. It has been extremely difficult for many central office and PBX switch makers to shift from analog to digital switches. Indeed, the most recent success of Northern Telecom against such entrenched competitors as AT&T, ITT, and Siemens is often attributed to the inability of these established firms to produce good quality digital switches.

The reluctance or inability of highly specialized companies to employ a breadth of technological knowledge often leads them to introduce products that evolve naturally out of their current technological base without regard for the needs and desires of their potential consumers. This is called technology-driven innovation, and it can be one of the most disastrous by-products of the expertise barrier. For any company to market a successful innovation, it must first astutely and objectively gauge market forces and adapt to them. In other words, it must be market-driven, because the ultimate acceptance of an innovation lies with the consumer. If an innovation fails to meet consumer needs, if it requires some undesirable change in usual consumption patterns, the consumer will reject it outright. An innovative company must therefore be flexible enough to upset established patterns of technological research and development to meet the demands of the marketplace. Unfortunately, this is an extremely difficult task for a highly specialized company, and the temptation to market innovations simply because they are compatible with the prevailing company technology can be overwhelming.

The failure of USCI to capture the DBS television market was, as we saw at the beginning of this chapter, the result of technology-driven innovation. USCI management had counted on their early entry into the field and their considerable expertise to ensure their success, but they failed to take one all-important factor into account: the consumer. Similar failures have plagued would-be innovators in a wide variety of products and services.

The diesel engine provides an excellent example of such a misguided strategy. For automobile manufacturers such as General Motors and Volkswagen, conversion from gasoline to diesel engines seemed the ideal means of capitalizing on a new consumer preference: fuel economy. It was certainly the most convenient means, for it presented no unusual technological challenge to the highly specialized design engineers. But, as always, the consumer had the last word, and that word was *no* for a number of reasons. First of all, diesel fuel was not as easily accessible to automobile drivers as gasoline. The 20,000 diesel fuel outlets in the United States represented a mere 14 percent of service stations operating in the country, and many of these outlets were geared to large volume truck sales and did not welcome automobiles. The diesel driver was thus faced with the knowledge that only one in seven stations would be able to fuel his car and many of these may not want his business. In addition, the diesel engine was noisy, smelly, and sometimes difficult to start. Its maintenance was quite different from that of the gasoline engine, and the customer had to be trained to operate it properly.

Automobile manufacturers introduced diesel engines for the worst of reasons: not because anyone really wanted to buy them, but because they required no significant disruption in established engineering routines. But however convenient the diesel engine was for the manufacturers to produce, it was inconvenient for potential buyers and, as a result, it fizzled after a brief success in the fuel-economy niche (see chapter 7).

Solutions

A high degree of technical specialization is a double-edged sword. It can generate great efficiency through the learning curve, but it can also either paralyze or severely misguide the process of innovation through the expertise barrier. But whether the result is poor innovation or no innovation at all, the cause is still the same: People with a vested interest in a highly specialized technology—technocrats—tend to be either unable or unwilling to disrupt established procedures radically enough to produce truly market-driven innovations. Thus far in this section, we have merely concentrated on defining the problem. But recognizing the enemy is only the first step. The solutions we recommend here should go a long way toward ensuring ultimate victory for the forces of change.

Skunk Works As Peters and Waterman discovered in a survey of excellent companies, one highly efficient way of encouraging innovative thinking is to organize technically talented people into an autonomous task force, called a skunk works, that is entirely free from the corporate structure, system of rewards, and even culture. This technique succeeds because it provides creative people with the freedom to experiment outside the constraining influence of established corporate behavior—and, more importantly, thought. Skunk works have been the prime avenue for successful innovations in such diverse areas as computer software, medical electronics, and even Mrs. Field's Cookies.

But the best example of skunk works involves IBM's extraordinary success in the personal computer (PC) business; it is a classic case history of how to overcome the specialization barrier in a large organization. The company was organized and driven by mainframe computer technology and by big business customers. In the existing organization, the development of the PC thus ran into a lot of internal resistance. IBM needed to develop a separate microprocessor that would be cost-effective. They had to design a computer at a price lower than their manufacturing expertise could handle. The solution was to create a separate, autonomous product team and give it the freedom to do what was necessary rather than worry about meeting the corporate structure and operations requirements.

The development and marketing of the PC broke some of the most respected traditions at IBM. First, the team bought the microprocessor chip from the outside rather than developing it within the company. Second, it decided to sell the personal computers through third-party distributors, which ran contrary to IBM's policy of direct sales to end-users. Third, the team designed the PC to be less a system and more a set of modular components, so that the customer could mix and match other manufacturers' peripherals. Finally, it encouraged small entrepreneurs to develop applications software, another significant departure from the IBM corporate culture.

A similar story is also told at Apple Computers. After the success of the Apple II series, the company was having difficulty developing more powerful and faster computers to regain the lead from IBM's PC. Many attempts from the same group of design engineers resulted in only mediocre products, and most of them failed, especially the Apple Lisa computer.

Steve Jobs, the founder of the company, decided that the best way to develop a new generation of personal computers was to organize a separate autonomous team that would focus exclusively on the new design and not worry about compatibility and potential cannibalization of Apple II computers. In fact, he stepped down from managing the business to lead the team. The result was the creation of the Macintosh line of personal computers, which focused on user friendliness, and which simplified the use of the keyboard by developing a mouse. Macintosh has been a very successful product line for Apple. In fact, it is only with the Macintosh line that Apple has finally succeeded in the business applications of personal computers, where IBM has dominated for many years.

Finally, AT&T has had difficulty in designing and marketing computers. When their B series of minicomputers was introduced, they were obsolete by at least five years. The series had very limited software support. The distribution was also very sketchy, and there was virtually no product support. This disaster occurred because AT&T tried to innovate and market computers in a manner very similar to how they operated the telephone business. Only recently have they decided to transfer all responsibility for the design and development of computers to Olivetti, the Italian office equipment and computer giant, in the hopes that this strategic alliance will encourage more innovation.

Research Alliances. It is becoming increasingly common for innovative companies to form strategic research alliances with individuals and organizations that wish to share their expertise for mutual profit. Many pharmaceutical and chemical companies, which have found it extremely difficult to innovate successfully, are now investing in research and development with the academic research community in biogenetics and bioengineering. Indeed, many universities are developing an infrastructure to attract such research alliances by forming semiprivate, autonomous research centers with corporations.

But research alliances need not be limited to companies with deep pockets and starving academics. A variety of organizations can profit from research alliances in which each member possesses a highly specialized skill that the other does not. The videotex business, for example, demands skills in database management, networking, and hardware, which are often not possessed by any one company alone. Thus, a productive research alliance in the videotex field could be formed by a telephone company, a software house, and a computer hardware company. In fact, it would be very useful to include one more partner who specializes in such specific applications as health care, commercial transactions, education, or entertainment.

Recently, a similar alliance has been formed among several different companies in developing and testing smart house technology, the inside wiring of homes in which the same outlet can be used interchangeably for telephone, computers, television, cable, and home appliances. The smart house consortium includes Whirlpool, AT&T, RCA, General Electric, the American Home Builders Association, the 3M Company, and the AMP Corporation.

Unlike skunk works, then, research alliances allow companies to maintain their established patterns of design engineering throughout the research and development process. The alliances simply provide creative combinations of these established patterns that afford the breadth of knowledge necessary for successful innovation.

Acquisitions. Another increasingly popular way that would-be innovators have successfully overcome the expertise barrier is by acquiring or merging with another organization that has the knowledge or experience the original company lacks. For example, when Sears management decided to expand into the field of retail financial services, they bought out Dean Witter, Coldwell Banker, and a commercial bank to acquire the necessary expertise. Similarly, American Express bought out IDS, Shearson/Lehman, and Firemen's Fund Insurance when they decided to go into financial services.

The same phenomenon is occurring in the retail food industry among volume-driven companies that wish to become single vendors to supply a wide range of products to supermarkets and convenience stores. Mergers to this end have taken place between Esmark and Beatrice, R.J. Reynolds and Nabisco, Nestle and Carnation, and Philip Morris and General Foods. There has also been a recent flurry of acquisitions and mergers in the advertising business among companies that hope to become one-stop suppliers of advertising, public relations, and direct marketing services.

Unfortunately, unwise acquisitions and mergers often create as many problems as they solve when the firmly entrenched management styles and corporate cultures of the two newlyweds clash. The recent disappointing experience of Kraft and Dart Industries, the dismantling of the Beatrice conglomerate, General Motors' acquisition of EDS, and Exxon's entry into the office automation market clearly indicate that mergers and acquisitions must be carefully researched and implemented if they are to result in successful innovation. A truly productive merger or acquisition allows the companies involved to overcome the expertise barrier by breaking out of their established patterns of technological development. All too many mergers and acquisitions, however, simply provide new barriers that double the impediments to effective change.

The Operations Barrier

A second major barrier to innovation—one closely related to the expertise barrier—is that of entrenched corporate operations. This barrier, like the previous one, is a matter of overspecialization and resistance to change; it simply occurs farther down the line, in production and assembly rather than research and development. Indeed, a company that is highly specialized in its technology is often equally specialized in its operations. This is a natural result of the experience curve. Innovation in such a company often involves changes not only in design engineering but also in materials procurement, manufacturing, and worker training as well—in short, operational changes. Nor are such changes merely minor inconveniences for the company. They often involve changing the intricate web of authority that draws the diverse strands of activity together into a functioning, and self-perpetuating, organization. Small wonder, then, that the more specialized and focused the organization, the less adaptable its operations are likely to be, for when all the strands of a web interconnect in the service of a single objective, the alteration of a single strand can threaten the unity and strength of the entire fabric. It is the fear of such disruption that leads to the expertise barrier in research and development and to the operations barrier in production and assembly.

By their very nature, then, companies with highly specialized operations face formidable barriers to innovation. Some innovate slowly, some not at all. For example, appliance companies have found it difficult to switch from metals to plastics in their manufacturing process and to integrate electronic controls into their products because both operational changes require significant modification of established patterns of manufacture, design, and worker training. Similar difficulties plagued Kodak in switching from movie cameras to video cameras, the U.S. automobile industry in switching from large to small cars, and hard disk manufacturers in switching to optical laser disks.

The operational barrier faced by traditional winemakers has been virtually insurmountable because of the deeply entrenched, almost ritual nature of their age-old craft and the extremely focused and specialized procedures involved. The raw materials required (grapes, chemicals), the blending and processing, not to mention the packaging and aging processes, are unique to winemaking. Naturally, the efficiency curve related to these highly technical and delicate processes is formidable. And it has been in place for centuries! The philosophy of the wine business is, quite simply, "If it ain't broke, don't fix it." As a result, recent product innovations such as light wine and wine coolers have been made by nontraditional and highly entrepreneurial firms rather than by the established leaders in the field.

Additionally, companies faced with operations barriers—like those faced with expertise barriers—are often tempted to market innovations that are operationally continuous rather than market-driven. The diesel defeat in the mass market, mentioned earlier, was at least as much a result of the operations barrier as it was of the expertise barrier. Diesel engines did not require major redesign of the production or assembly process, and

The Specialization Trap

it was therefore all too easy to market them without due regard for potential consumer response.

Another excellent example of a product that was marketed primarily because its manufacture posed few operational problems for its producers is the dishwasher. A large number of households now use dishwashers, but for many years they were expensive white elephants for such appliance manufacturers as GE, Whirlpool, Westinghouse, and Sears, who made them because they *could*. These companies had all successfully designed and produced machines for washing clothes, so they had no difficulty producing machines for washing dishes.

The problem was that consumers did not particularly want dishwashers. First, many traditional homemakers felt that the automatic dishwasher provided little advantage over long-established dishwashing aids: husbands and teenagers. Second, they considered dishwashers luxury items that would reflect poorly on their ability as homemakers. Third, they did not believe that dishwashers would do a thorough job or be particularly expedient, since dishes had to be specially prepared before the machine could work effectively. And, finally, many consumers felt that dishwashers were simply too expensive: They even required special dishes! No wonder only one household in eight had a dishwasher in the 1960s. Marketed in response to producer ability rather than consumer demand, the dishwasher would have to await the cultural changes of the 1980s to come into its own, no thanks to its originators.

Solutions

Although the operations barrier is similar in both cause and result to the expertise barrier, the task of overcoming it requires somewhat different strategies aimed, naturally enough, at production and assembly rather than research and development. Nonetheless, all these strategies share the same fundamental purpose: to help companies break out of the established patterns of behavior that either retard or prevent successful innovation.

Separate Operations. One extremely valuable strategy in overcoming the operations barrier is to start a fresh, separate operation divorced from current physical facilities, workers, and even management. This alternative functions rather like a skunk works in that it permits innovative activities to flourish without the constraining influence of entrenched routine and, at the same time, allows established operational processes to continue without disruption.

The recent announcement by General Motors that it was starting a new automobile division—Saturn—is a good example of establishing a separate organization to produce different cars than those made by the existing division. The Saturn project is often referred to as a management laboratory, in which the business unit is explicitly charged with the responsibility of innovative design, manufacture, distribution, selling, and service operations. Indeed, GM hopes that this autonomous unit can generate ideas that, when transferred to the traditional divisions, will make GM more competitive against foreign competition.

Modified Operations. A second possible solution, most useful in those industries where physical plant and land resources are of a significant size and scope, is the modification of existing operations to facilitate innovation. For example, the automobile industry is modifying its existing assembly plants to incorporate factory automation. Telephone companies are upgrading their central offices with digital switches and the local loop with fiber optics. And, finally, both Hilton and Marriott are buying out grand old hotels and modernizing them. Clearly this solution does not safeguard both innovative and established operations as meticulously as does the previous option. But, especially when the established operation is outdated, this kind of

The Specialization Trap

organization-wide modification is often the most desirable route to successful innovation. The integration of new operational procedures must, however, be performed with extreme care to avoid lowering the efficiency of continuing operations or even disrupting and dispiriting the entire corporate culture.

The growing use of robots and vision systems in the manufacture of automobiles provides another illustration of the power of operations barriers. Chrysler Corporation had to set up an entirely new type of assembly line at its Windsor (Ontario, Canada) assembly plant to facilitate the use of robots with "vision." Using newly designed computer hardware and laser technology, the robots are provided with an "eye." This eye replaces the vision of the human inspectors and can tirelessly detect the smallest defects in car doors before they are fitted onto the auto body. Some of these vision systems, aided by the development of low-cost, powerful microprocessors, can detect and measure complex black-and-white images (usually in 64 shades of gray) in a fraction of a second!

Chrysler is also installing automated welding systems of eight robots to weld stamped panels into K-car bodies. In order to switch to automated production, Chrysler has had to shift from a labor base to a capital base. All this meant a total deviation from prior known and established patterns of manual assembly line production, where parts were moved from one shop floor to the next, a sample from each batch was tested for quality control, and the final assembly was done by human labor. Of course, this massive change in operations was made possible because Chrysler was in financial trouble and therefore could negotiate with its workers to accommodate the change.

Selectively Modified Operations. Some of the dangers of organization-wide operational modification can be minimized by, when possible, limiting modifications to a discrete portion of the organization. Depending on whether innovation will more directly involve upstreaming or downstreaming operations, modifications can be focused specifically on either supplier or customer operations. By thus targeting change to the area most in need of it, the innovative company can achieve some of the dual-safeguarding advantages provided in the separate-operations solution. For example, it has been relatively easier to automate stand-alone retail stores or branches than a total corporation. And, similarly, it has been easier to automate physical distribution at the warehouse than at the factory or the retail level. In both cases, innovative operations are protected from established ones, and vice versa. Nevertheless, it is still important to integrate new procedures with care to avoid smaller-scale, but still potentially damaging, effects on efficiency and morale.

THE ENVIRONMENTAL CHALLENGE

Even a company that is both determined to innovate and adaptable enough in its technological and operational procedures to do so successfully may still face formidable barriers in its environment that inhibit effective innovation. But these barriers are not Acts of God or "circumstances beyond our control." They are clearly definable and solvable problems. Specifically, they include the *resource barrier*, the *regulation barrier*, and the *market access barrier*. And, although their sources are external to the corporation, the most effective responses to each can and must come from within. In this section, we will examine these barriers in detail and suggest tested and eminently workable solutions to each.

The Resource Barrier

It is undeniable that nothing so successfully discourages any business venture as insufficient funds. This factor is as potent in

The Environmental Challenge

setting up a lemonade stand as it is in marketing a revolutionary computer system, and it is especially influential in determining whether an innovation will ever see the light of day. Few organizations have deep pockets. Only for a handful of cash-rich corporations is money truly "no object" in the process of innovation; hence, the great destructive power of the resource barrier and the wide expanse of its influence.

Specifically stated, the ability of the resource barrier to obstruct the process of innovation is determined by the borrowing power (i.e., current debt-to-equity ratio) of the corporation. Indeed, many international business experts attribute Japan's extraordinarily successful innovation drives to its three-to-one debt-to-equity ratio as compared to the one-to-one ratio generally required of U.S. companies.

U.S. investment bankers have been reluctant to provide long-term debt to public corporations above and beyond the 50–50 ratio. They fear that a U.S. company will incur significant interest costs, which the margins of its products are unlikely to bear. In Japan, on the other hand, investment banks commonly provide long-term loans, especially to the large Japanese conglomerates, such as Mitsubishi, Mitsui, Sumitomo, and Matsushita, that have three to four times the equity of a single corporation. The banks do not worry about the interest costs because these companies obtain very low-cost capital from the Japanese government as an incentive to go into specified targeted industries such as automobiles, consumer electronics, ship building, and steel mills.

Many examples, both familiar and obscure, grimly illustrate the power of this barrier. Perhaps the most dramatic comes from the airlines industry. Freddie Laker had a successful and innovative strategy of expanding Atlantic air traffic by offering low prices and standby fares. He was highly successful in generating business between London and New York because the low fares were especially attractive to college and high school students and to tourists. He decided to expand his operation to many other U.S. cities rather than concentrate on the New York–London route.

Unfortunately, markets from other cities such as Detroit, Dallas, Houston, and Orlando did not have the numbers to fill up the DC-10 aircrafts. Without the revenue from passengers to cover the costs of added planes and personnel, Laker could not meet expenses. Short on resources, he was forced to declare bankruptcy.

A less well-publicized story with a similar moral is taking place in the world of high tech. A number of telecommunications suppliers are experiencing financial difficulties as they try to shift from analog to digital technologies for central office and private branch exchange (PBX) markets. In fact, ITT recently abandoned its efforts to develop the digital switch because it didn't have the funds or the inclination to invest in the project. And even the German giant, Siemens, has decided to join with GTE to minimize the financial risk.

The same phenomenon can be observed in the long-distance telephone market. Even though it is a deregulated business, most common carriers other than MCI and AT&T, such as Sprint and Alnet, are finding it financially difficult to build their own interexchange facilities. Recently, GTE sold the Sprint business to United Telephone to form a joint venture called U.S. Sprint.

In contrast, one would expect financial barriers to be considerably less formidable in certain common consumer nondurables. We all know of many "Mom and Pop" success stories. However, it requires more than $15 million to nationally promote and distribute a packaged good in the United States—a sum often beyond the limits of many European companies as well as many small, regional, U.S. firms.

In many instances, an innovation generated by a highly entrepreneurial company is exploited by the large companies. For example, in the beer industry, a number of local breweries had tried to introduce diet beer, but with no success. It took massive amounts of advertising and distribution by Miller beer after its acquisition by Philip Morris to successfully introduce its Lite beer. Indeed, the beer industry has consistently demonstrated that local popularity does not translate into national success without financial clout. Falstaff, Olympia, Pabst, and even Coors have learned this hard lesson: A distinctive product is not enough.

Despite the enormous market size and potential growth of the industry, a number of companies in the health care field have hit the resource barrier when trying to provide innovative services such as health maintenance organizations (HMOs), group clinics, and 24-hour emergency centers. Recently, Maxicare bought out two other HMOs to create the economy of scale necessary to survive.

Solutions

There are a number of ways to expand financing of an innovative offering and thus break through the resource barrier.

License Agreements. The first and perhaps the most common strategy is to license the innovation to others. Sony Corporation learned this approach the hard way. It pioneered the VCR technology and established the beta format. Unfortunately, the beta format, which is technically superior to VHS, was not blessed by the Ministry of International Trade and Industries (MITI). Most other Japanese companies, most notably Matsushita (maker of the Panasonic and National brands), Hitachi, and Sharp, decided to manufacture and market the VHS format in order to make it more affordable to the mass market. As a result, Sony lost the VCR market even though it had a better quality product.

Sony has, however, recently changed its strategy. Rather than take the entire responsibility for producing and marketing its innovative 8-mm. video cameras, it has decided to license the technology to more than 150 manufacturers on a worldwide basis so that Sony does not have to solely support the market development and the manufacturing costs.

The parallel approach to licensing is franchising. Franchising is a contractual agreement by which one firm offers its unique product/service idea for distribution to other companies or individuals for a fee. At the same time, the original, innovating firm creates a national image, ensures quality standards, and makes sure each franchise follows the contractual terms for procurement, marketing, selling, and service. A number of innovative products and services over the years have been successfully introduced by franchising. The best success stories for franchising have been McDonald's in the hamburger business, Snap-on-Tools in industrial tools distribution, Ace Hardware and IGA Supermarkets in retailing, and Century 21 in real estate.

Consortiums. A consortium is a cooperative or joint venture in which several potentially competitive and complementary companies get together to develop a common technology so that it becomes the de facto technical standard.

The smart house project referred to earlier is a very good example of a consortium. The objective is to develop an innovative home wiring technology and test it in new homes. The new system consists of a single wire that runs throughout the house. Each outlet is capable of accepting appliances, electronics, telephones, and cable television. At present, homes need separate outlets and systems and different holes and locations.

Furthermore, each outlet has several unique features. First of all, electricity is not dispensed until the appliance is plugged in. Second, the single system distributes the correct amount of energy for each appliance rather than the standard voltage. Third, it eliminates electric shock. You can put your finger in the outlet and there is no current.

In order to dispense current, the system requires each appliance (television, telephone, etc.) to have an intelligent mi-

The Environmental Challenge

croprocessor to inform the outlet who it is: "I am the television," "I am the iron," and so on. Finally, it does not work if the appliance is defective. The smart house is one of the major breakthroughs in inside wiring since the discovery of electricity.

A consortium is necessary in this sort of project for several reasons. First, the projects are too costly for any one company. Second, they are too complex for one company to solve. Expertise must be garnered from different disciplines. Third, the consortium facilitates the establishment of a common agreement as to what the new generation of technical standards is.

The consortium idea was also employed by the International Telecommunications Union to produce the ISDN standards in telecommunications. The Union organized the Consultative Committee on International Telecommunications and Telegraphs (CCITT) to create the standards.

Venture Capital. A third approach to breaking down the resource barrier is to invite venture capital into the operation. The role of venture capital in developing innovative offerings is well known. In recent years, as a matter of fact, venture capital seems to have become *the* solution for a lack of adequate resources. Unfortunately, venture capital suffers from some of the same corporate culture problems manifested in acquisitions and mergers. First of all, venture capitalists are often unfamiliar with the technical and operational barriers that hinder the innovative process. Venture capitalists are not committed to any one technology. They are really investment bankers specializing in new ventures that are high risk and therefore outside the parameters of the standard banks. Second, they must play the odds. As pure investors, they are interested only in their financial returns. They have learned from experience that it is much better to spread the risk over several ventures rather than invest heavily in one venture only. Therefore, they are unable or unwilling to commit more than the minimum. Finally, they tend to impose financial controls that may or may not be beneficial to the venture.

The Regulation Barrier

Regulation can take several forms, and most industries are subject to at least one of them. The first type of regulation is industry self-regulation, which is normally limited to codes of business practice and business ethics as expressed by an industry, trade, or professional association. Perhaps the best known instances of self-regulation come from such professional service organizations as the American Medical Association or the American Bar Association. Such self-policing is also prevalent in agriculture, manufacturing, and practically all other types of industries.

The second type is government regulation of both a company's internal operations and its market operations. Government regulators are concerned with product safety, occupational safety, antitrust violations, and trade practices. Federal agents work out of the Federal Aviation Administration (FAA), the Department of Justice (DOJ), the Environmental Protection Agency (EPA), and the Federal Trade Commission (FTC).

The FAA regulates the aviation industry by certifying aircraft, setting maintenance standards, controlling air space, and overseeing the commercial aviation business. Their primary mission is product safety and passenger safety.

The DOJ is in charge of regulating competition. They watch each industry and determine whether competition is minimized by any company that is becoming too dominant. They broke up the Bell System for this reason, and they filed a lengthy suit against IBM. In the old days, they broke the Standard Oil monopoly. They also review every acquisition and merger case. Recently, this has been the most active field of their involvement.

The FTC regulates trade practices of all industries, including advertising, mail order, distribution, and all other trade activities except product safety. Their biggest impact has been on advertising, packaging, and product labeling. They focus on information disclosure, claims, and so on.

A third type of regulation is limited to utility monopolies, such as water, gas, electricity, and telephone service. The fundamental thrust here is rate regulation, in which prices and products are approved by a government agency. The Public Utility Commission (PUC), for example, in each state determines what telecommunications services can be offered and what prices can be charged.

The fourth type of regulation relates to patents and trademarks. The patent office grants individuals certain rights for being innovative. Every inventor or designer can file for a patent. Once the patent rights are given, the innovator has 14 years to develop the product and market it commercially. The idea is to protect people from imitators with better resources who might exploit the innovation and deny the innovator the commercial opportunity. Patents have, however, become a major regulatory barrier to firms that make pharmaceutical, agricultural, and specialty chemicals because their better imitations or second cousin innovations are kept off the market for a number of years.

Whatever the worthy motives may be for regulating industry, the basic truth remains that the more regulated an industry or a company, the greater the barrier to innovation. Although regulation can be an agent for change—as in the enforcement of higher safety standards—in practice it tends to preserve the status quo. And business as usual is the enemy of creative innovation. The power of the regulatory barrier should become evident with a few illustrations.

Consider the case of consumable packaged goods. At present, there is a strong legal bias against treating prepared foods with radiation. Although irradiation of foods as a technology has been in existence for many years and is in widespread use in Europe and elsewhere, it has run into a regulatory barrier in the United States. The Food and Drug Administration (FDA) has been extremely cautious and unwilling to encourage irradiation. According to the proponents of this new food preservation technology, irradiation is actually safer than the present food preservatives, additives, and even flavor enhancers such as salt and sugar. However, perhaps due to the fear of negative public opinion, the FDA has only recently permitted the use of irradiation technology on a very limited basis in raw food materials such as grains, vegetables, and fruits. As a result, a new generation of technology for food preservation with a better performance–price ratio is not likely to become a commercial reality for some time to come.

The regulation barrier is also very formidable in many service industries. The most recent examples can be found in the restrictions on financial services. In the United States, the unit banking system has traditionally been enforced in most states. This means that a bank is not allowed to have branches beyond a given geographical area, even within a state, although banking is statewide in some states. Only recently have we seen the emergence of interstate banking, and true national banking seems to be only a distant reality.

In contrast, Japanese and most European banks do not face such restrictions. Consequently, U.S. banking has remained backward. Most transactions are limited to local interbanking, local deposits, and local lending. Indeed, check clearinghouses and fund transfer procedures in the United States are at least one generation behind European banks. European banks have automated their check clearing and fund transfer transactions among banks as well as between customer and bank. For example, you can deposit money directly in another business or personal account (called a GIRO account) for practically all transactions without writing checks. In the United States, this practice has only recently been available, and it is limited to payroll and

The Environmental Challenge

social security checks. Also, as a result of cooperation, balances among the banks are cleared instantly rather than over a period of days.

There are numerous examples of barriers to innovation in the health care industry as well, ranging from the certification of new drugs to the development of cancer cures. All medications and treatments require years of testing on animals and clinical evaluation on humans before they will be approved by the government—specifically, the FDA. In fact, many pharmaceutical and medical electronics companies introduce new products and services in foreign countries first because regulation barriers are much lower than in the United States. Recently, for instance, Eli Lily decided to test its new arthritis drug in England because it was easier. Also, many embryo implant experiments (including test tube babies) are permitted in foreign countries but frowned upon here.

Finally, as part of the divestiture of the Bell Operating Companies (BOCs), AT&T agreed with the government that the BOCs should be restricted from entering three lines of businesses: information services, long distance calls, and manufacturing telephone equipment. A number of local network-based innovations are currently possible but cannot enter the marketplace because of that agreement. We do not now have, for instance, electronic yellow pages and certain database and transaction services that could be valuable to consumers and profitable for the BOCs as well.

Solutions

Remove the Barrier. A number of solutions are possible to minimize or eliminate regulatory hindrances to innovation. The most radical solution is to abolish the regulation by legislation. This approach has been adopted in such formerly regulated monopolies as airlines, trucking, and railways. Recently, one of the regional holding companies created as a result of the divestiture of the Bell System has used this strategy very effectively in several states to obtain its freedom from local regulation.

Change the Barrier. A second solution is to shift the regulatory jurisdiction from one agency to another. For example, it is possible to go from local to state and from state to federal jurisdictions. Many people are suggesting that the cable industry will not introduce innovative products and services until regulation is shifted from the local to the national arena. Of course, the reverse is also possible. The New Federalism proposed by President Reagan is an attempt to shift the burden of social regulation from federal to state jurisdictions. Several years earlier, the Supreme Court decided that morality standards should be set by each local community, not nationally. Therefore, it is up to local communities to determine what is pornographic. Recently, sex magazines such as *Hustler* have been banned in some communities as pornographic, although they are freely available in other places.

Bypass the Barrier. A third approach to lowering the regulatory barriers is reorganization. In many cases, this strategy requires forming a holding company with the freedom to offer product or service innovations not allowed the regulated entity. Reorganization is very common in the banking business, and it is becoming more prevalent in the telecommunications and health care industries. In banking, reorganization means creating a holding company that then owns several banks in different locations. This way, a large degree of bank consolidation takes place in several states, especially in the Midwest, where banks face more restrictions on the location of branch offices.

Regional telephone companies after the AT&T divestiture created a separate enterprise corporation in charge of all nonregulated businesses to accommodate the current restriction that the regulated local exchange should not subsidize the nonregulated businesses. The latter include telephone equipment, cellular mobile phones, the *Yellow Pages*, private networks, maintenance and repair, and international businesses.

Some corporations even register their assets in countries famous for low regulation barriers. For example, many companies register their ships in different countries or establish corporate headquarters in Luxembourg, Monaco, or Switzerland to escape more vigorous regulation at home.

The Market Access Barrier

Market access bottlenecks include such things as the lack of availability of shelf space in supermarkets for new, innovative products, or embedded technologies in computers or digital phone exchanges that make it difficult for customers to switch products. They appear in physical distribution, in customer support services, or in regulation. Market access barriers refer, in general, to all impediments that keep innovations from reaching receptive customers.

Market access barriers more often block small market share companies than market leaders. The smaller the market share, the greater the barrier.

The recent cola wars between Coca-Cola and Pepsi-Cola have clearly demonstrated how market access barriers can loom large for smaller companies. These two market leaders have virtually shut out other soft drink companies such as RC Cola, Dr Pepper, and even 7-Up at several distribution points: independent bottlers, vending machines, supermarkets, and even restaurants and fast food chains. There is only so much space in any of these outlets, and now that the Big Two offer so many more variations (without sugar and/or caffeine, with cherry flavor, etc.) the squeeze is even tighter. Since the public demands Coke and Pepsi, the smaller brands get pushed out.

Coke and Pepsi's physical dominance in the soft drink marketplace is obvious. But there are other less obvious examples of distribution clout that erect barriers for smaller, weaker products. R.J. Reynolds, for instance, owns almost all the cigarette racks in the supermarkets; Kraft manages all the supermarket dairy cases. Consider the added difficulty of marketing an innovative tobacco or dairy product not made by one of those two giants.

Perhaps the most prevalent and well understood market access barriers appear in international trade. Each country has its own trade barriers, which make it difficult for innovative products and services to cross national boundaries. Most trade barriers are consciously erected by governments to protect local interests or to minimize balance of payment problems.

Japan has the greatest reputation for strong trade barriers. Very few products from the United States or Europe can be imported into Japan. Ironically, one of the most effective of international trade barriers was constructed by France against Japanese VCRs (an innovative product the French could not duplicate). France permitted all Japanese VCRs to land only at one port. The port, furthermore, employed only one inspector. The inspector was instructed to go slow in his duties so that no more than 10 to 12 VCRs per day could enter the country.

The United States also has a number of ways to keep foreign competition out. We are, for instance, very strict about agricultural imports. We have also recently imposed heavy duties on forest products from Canada because the government believes that Canada is dumping in U.S. markets and putting domestic companies at a disadvantage. In addition, we have put a quota on the importation of textiles and clothing from many Third World countries, including Taiwan, Singapore, and South Korea. In the spring of 1987, we also imposed severe tariffs on certain Japanese electronic goods, such as television sets and microchips.

Strictly on the domestic front, examples abound of the entrenched keeping out the new. The dominant position of IBM in the mainframe business has, for instance, made it very difficult for several other computer manufacturers to reach the market even though they have innovative products and services. IBM's preeminence stems from excellent support services. Computer retailers constantly need assistance when software or hardware fail. They are reluctant to consider other companies and their product/services because they do not want to alienate IBM as a supplier.

An overwhelming leadership position has also helped the Boeing Company, and for much the same reason: Boeing provides strong technical support to an industry (airlines) that needs it. As a result, Boeing enjoys a lion's share of the commercial aircraft market. Consequently, innovative aircrafts such as Lockheed's L-1011 and the Airbus have had trouble penetrating the U.S. market. Their poor sales do not reflect the product quality.

The embedded technological position of the larger firms is also a major barrier to market access for new, innovative offerings. The first company in with computerized ordering, for instance, has an advantage. Federal Express takes advantage of its computer tracking system to encourage its biggest and best customers to locate their parts inventory in Memphis (Federal's headquarters) where it can be managed by Federal. The parts manager sends daily messages via a dedicated terminal about which parts should be shipped to whom. Once the customer is locked into the computerized shipping, it becomes very difficult for the competition to offer innovative products or programs and lure him or her away from Federal.

The local telephone companies also create market access barriers for their competitors. It is virtually impossible for anyone else to provide the local loop from the customer's home or office to the telephone exchange. This is particularly true for mass market residential and small business customers. Therefore, alternate technologies such as shared tenant services, smart buildings, teleports, satellite dishes, and even cellular mobile telephone systems have not made the inroads they should have against the copper wire technology.

Solutions

There are several ways companies can break through market access barriers. In plain language, they can follow the "If you can't beat 'em, join 'em" path (forming alliances), build their own ballpark (distribution channels), or get help from the inside (marketing).

Forming Alliances. The first and probably easiest approach is to align with the dominant vendor. For example, Michelin entered the U.S. market by selling its radial tires to Sears, which at one time had a bigger market share than Goodyear, Firestone, and B.F. Goodrich combined. Similarly, the Japanese succeeded in the automobile business by distributing their cars through General Motors dealers. Finally, many peripheral and software companies have learned to align with IBM by making IBM compatible products as well as by selling to IBM as an original equipment manufacturer.

Distribution Channels. A second solution is for the blocked firm to develop its own distribution system. This is a very costly approach, but sometimes it is the only way to penetrate a blocked market. Avon Cosmetics and Tupperware both felt they had to create their own distribution and selling organizations rather than rely on the department stores. In a related tack, Clinique cosmetics insisted on managing the retail floor space for its cosmetics because it didn't believe department store personnel could properly inform and educate customers about the uniqueness of their cosmetics. In general, the more proprietary the product or service, the more likely it is that dedicated distribution will succeed.

A more limited version of this strategy is available to smaller innovative companies. They can use telemarketing and direct marketing programs to, in effect, create their own distribution system outside traditional channels.

Marketing. Finally, it is possible to jump over the barriers by adopting a pull marketing strategy; that is, one can tap the power of the people on the other side of the barrier—the customers. Japanese companies advertise in India for their consumer electronics products such as televisions, VCRs, and stereo systems even though the Indian government does not allow imports. It is estimated that more than half a million Japanese VCRs are, nevertheless, in India—virtually all of them brought into the country by tourists or by smugglers! Pull marketing is especially important if the customer is unsure of how to procure the product or service. Japanese companies don't tell Indian consumers how to smuggle, but they do help the owners once the machines are in the country. Advertisements in local newspapers and magazines reassure the consumer that Japanese products are of the best quality and that they are easy to repair in India if something goes wrong. The ads also list authorized Indian service agents. It is easy to dodge the market access barrier in this instance through the power of advertising, promotion, and publicity.

SUMMARY

The five major barriers to innovation inherent in the structure of the corporation must be recognized and understood before the innovation can be brought to market successfully. The barriers of expertise and operations present problems of specialization in technology and organization. Resources, regulation, and market access barriers reflect problems in the business environment.

Specialized expertise generates technology-driven innovations, like DBS television, that fail in the marketplace. Firms have been able to break down this barrier through skunk works, research alliances, and acquisitions. Similarly, resistance to change in operations occurs from overspecialization in production and assembly. Again, innovations are produced because they are easy—like the dishwasher—and not because they respond to market needs. The solutions here are to create separate operations or modify existing ones.

Resource problems arise when a firm has insufficient borrowing power to sustain the innovation in the market, as with Freddie Laker's airline. When faced with this barrier, innovative companies can offer licensing agreements, form consortiums, or seek venture capital. Regulation thwarts innovation in businesses as diverse as banking and packaged goods. Firms can respond by reorganizing or by attempting to change regulations or their jurisdiction. Finally, difficulties in reaching customers constitute market access barriers, most often encountered by small firms like RC Cola up against the giants (Coke and Pepsi). Blocked companies can form alliances with larger corporations that have market clout, develop their own distribution system, or adopt a pull marketing strategy.

Corporate barriers are tough, but beatable. In the next chapter, we will look at an even more formidable hurdle to marketing innovations: structural customer resistance.

Bohn, J. "Robotics: Gearing Up for Japan's Threat." *Business Marketing*, May 1984.

Duffy, H.A. "Deregulating Safely." *USA Today*, July, 1984, 54–56.

McLean, J. "IBM to Adopt 3rd Party Financing Plan." *Business News*, April 26, 1982, 24.

Robertson, T.S., & Ward, S. "Management Lesson from Airline Regulation." *Harvard Business Review*, Jan.–Feb. 1983, 40.

Williams, M. "Slow Liftoff for Satellite to Home TV." *Fortune*, March 5, 1984, 100.

"Average Effective Patent Life for New Entries in 1980: 7.5 Years." *American Druggist*, Oct. 1981.

"Competitive Drive: A Hot New Computer Technology Begins to Draw a Crowd." *Barron's National Business and Financial Weekly*, Aug. 30, 1982, 12–13.

References

"School Computers Score At Last." *Business Week*, July 27, 1981, 66–68.

"The Big News at AT&T Isn't Its Personal Computer." *Business Week*, July 9, 1984, 80–82.

"The Speed-Up in Automation." *Business Week*, Aug. 3, 1981, 58–67.

"Machines that Can See: Here Comes a New Generation." *Business Week*, Jan. 9, 1984, 69–73.

"Canada: A Licensing Law that Hurts U.S. Drugmakers." *Business Week*, March 1, 1982, 34.

"Deregulation Still Has a Long Way to Go." *Business Week*, Aug. 23, 1983, 74.

"A Bipartisan Swing Back to More Regulation." *Business Week*, May 30, 1983, 74.

"Trademarks: Why Companies Guard Them More Tightly." *Chemical Weekly*, Jan. 13, 1982, 30–33.

"Now the Generic Drugs Can Be Look-Alikes Too." *Chemical Week*, June 30, 1982, 41–42.

3
Customer Barriers to Innovation

Consumer advocates such as Ralph Nader have been lobbying for more safety devices in automobiles—like the air bag. Conceived without much fanfare in the early 1970s, the air bag has since gone through a traumatic nursing period. The incorporation of air bags into the design of automobiles has not been as easy for the manufacturers as has its predecessor, seat belts. Seat belts could be easily installed with a buckle and strap arrangement that needed no special changes in either the body framework or the seats.

Air bags, on the other hand, need a few auxiliary features that the automobile manufacturers must consider. First, the front fenders must be fitted with an electronic sensing device that would release the air bags. This entails trial testing and acceptance of electronics that are compatible with the automobiles. Second, the dashboard design must be modified to incorporate the air bags. This, too, means additional costs for research, design, and manufacture—all for a substitute for seat belts, which are efficient by themselves.

Even if the problems could be solved, it is not clear whether consumers would like the styling or even accept this new safety measure. First, automobiles with air bags cost more than those without by as much as $500 per car. Second, the air bags are meant for only front-seat passengers and thus provide no special benefit to those who are in the rear of the car, especially in a rear-side accident. Third, while seat belts are easy to operate, air bags could be cumbersome. As soon as the fender of the automobile comes into contact with any object, the air bags instantly balloon out of the inlets built in the dashboard. The problem, though, is that air bags are triggered into action even at the slightest contact, not necessarily a major impact or collision. Once the air bags are released, returning them to their original receptacle is not an easy task. Many people have had to seek the help of their dealers to restore the air bags to their ready position.

Customers thus have to put up with yet another maintenance problem, and are therefore unwilling to accept the product. In short, air bags are good for car owners, who are interested. But the innovation has not been accepted by all consumers because of the disruptive features inherent in the technology. Until those customer-aggravating qualities are eliminated by superior design or the use of air bags is made mandatory, it is unlikely that air bags will be widely accepted in this country.

The air bag saga illustrates the strength of the barriers to innovation that can be erected by corporations and by customers. Although structural barriers inherent in corporations can be quite formidable, as we saw in the previous chapter, those impediments generated outside the business, by customers, offer even stronger resistance to successful innovation. The reasons encompass free will, ignorance, and diversity.

Why are customer barriers more powerful? First, the customers can exercise their free will. A corporation has less control over the customers, unless it is a monopoly. Even in the worst monopoly situation, the customers can always decide not to buy from anyone (and, if necessary, to make it themselves). The telecommunications industry provides numerous examples of customers selecting this option. Many large corporate customers, including the government, have decided to build and manage their own private networks rather than buy the service from the telephone companies. Similarly, owners of office buildings offer shared phone services to their small business tenants as a value-added service.

Second, customers often do not know the capabilities of a new technology and, therefore, cannot understand its potential benefits. For example, the potential of the personal computer is enormous, at least to the same degree as the telephone and the television. However, most consumers, including those in corporations, use PCs primarily as word processors and then complain that they overspent their money.

The problem of the customer's technical incompetence is so great that we do not recommend using standard survey research methods to assess customer interest in a new technology. Instead, it becomes increasingly necessary to provide free trials so that potential customers can actually use the technology in their natural environment. Observing what they *actually do* with it is much better than asking what they would *like to do* with a product that breaks new ground.

Finally, customers are represented by a large number of stakeholders, ranging from social critics to consumer advocates to government agencies. Trying to induce this naturally skeptical audience to adopt an innovation often elicits strong reactions, especially if the new technology either is not fully developed or has potential unwanted side effects. Over the years, the chemical industry has had to contend with this reaction. Consider what has happened with agricultural chemicals (DDT), roofing materials (asbestos), cigarettes (tar and nicotine), coffee (caffeine), and drugs such as Thalidomide (birth defects). This historical record has a very unfortunate side effect of its own: Innovation is increasingly considered such an economic risk that corporations become paralyzed by objections from their legal departments. Obviously, dangerous side effects such as those just listed should elicit a negative consumer (and corporate) response. These extreme cases, unfortunately, generate a negative aura around all innovative products, particularly those involving new chemicals. That attitude is something with which innovators must contend, not something from which they must flee.

At the same time, it must be recognized that customers do not necessarily resist a particular innovation because they dislike it. They resist because innovations create change and structural discontinuities, that is, disruptions of life patterns that have become comfortable. Remember that a true innovation represents a significantly different way of satisfying the same need or of performing the same function. It is a substitute technology, not just another variation of the same product. It is more than just "new and improved."

What is needed, therefore, is an understanding of the disruptions innovations cause and a customer-driven philosophy so that innovation efforts can be channeled in a direction that minimizes change in the customers' current practices and values. To that end, we have identified five areas of customer concern that are sufficiently strong to raise up barriers to the adoption of innovations. These barriers can be grouped into two categories: those that are primarily practical or functional and those that are essentially psychological. The first set has to do with usage patterns, economic values, and risks. The second set is concerned with cultural tradition and image. We will discuss each in turn with illustrations from different sectors of the economy. As in chapter 2, we will also offer solutions to the problems the barriers pose.

PRACTICAL OBJECTIONS

The Usage Barrier

Perhaps the most common reason for customer resistance to an innovation is that it is not compatible with existing workflows, practices, and/or habits. Innovations that require significant changes in the daily routine require a long market development process, often extending over generations. Indeed, many well known innovations such as television, computers, and telephones, were invented decades before their successful commercialization and often required repackaging in a way suitable to the customer's operations.

In addition, once a new technology is accepted and established, the next wave of innovations faces the same customer usage barrier as the original. In the computer field, for instance, since IBM's successful introduction of hardware and software technologies, most efforts to introduce alternative hardware and software architectures have met with customer resistance. This is not surprising. Once a customer's organization is comfortable with the IBM systems, it is very difficult to retrain either the professionals in data processing or the various other users throughout the organization.

The same phenomenon has emerged in the personal computer business. Unless other manufacturers create IBM-compatible hardware and software, their products are very difficult to sell. Zenith, NCR, Hewlett-Packard, Data General, and a host of other computer manufacturers have tried to offer alternate technologies. All have met with only limited success. The only possible threat to IBM dominance is Unix, from AT&T. Unix has so many advantages over IBM's operating systems that *over a long period of time and with considerable commitment and effort*, customers could shift their use of computer hardware and software systems.

Although computers are a dynamic product, they are, in a sense, an old story. A new story concerning the introduction of technological innovations is unfolding in factory automation and robotics. U.S. automobile companies are highly motivated to meet foreign competition by adopting foreign competitive practices. They are finding it extremely difficult to switch to robots, however, since the move requires worker and management retraining, and involves numerous operational headaches in implementation.

It is our belief that robots will see very limited use in the factory in the near future. Unlike machine tools, robots will be only special purpose machines. They are likely to be used in situations where the human body and mind are incapable of functioning—as in hazardous areas of extreme hot or cold temperatures—or where very complicated calculations must be made in a short time, or where the precision required for quality assurance is beyond the capabilities of human beings.

The service sector also offers several cases of usage barriers to innovations. Consider video teleconferencing, an innovation that allows people to meet face to face without the trouble and expense of travel. Unfortunately, video teleconferencing requires significant changes in workflows, practices, and habits. It has to be planned ahead, people have to go to specific locations away from their offices, documents must be prepared and distributed ahead of time, and the flow of communication has to be orchestrated. In addition, most managers feel uncomfortable in front of the cameras and start to behave as if they were on stage!

The same problem of usage discontinuity seems to be the fundamental reason why most commuters do not carpool or vanpool to work. It requires significant change in the daily routine. Carpoolers must leave the office or factory at the same time everyday, must sit in the car or in the van in the same way, and may not be able to do the things they are in the habit of doing while driving alone, such as listening to a favorite radio station, stopping at a store, or making personal calls on the car phone. Furthermore, carpooling requires compatibility with other carpoolers' punctuality, manners, communication styles, and even personal grooming habits!

A companion case to the carpool might be the electric car; it, too, affronts our driving habits. To begin with, the owner must

Practical Objections

recharge the batteries overnight. Once on the road, the maximum speed is far below the gasoline engine cars, the acceleration is less powerful, and the driving range is highly limited. Furthermore, accessible service stations are not equipped to casually and quickly recharge the batteries, make repairs and do routine maintenance, or provide emergency assistance. It is unlikely, therefore, that electric cars will ever be accepted by the majority of motorists, despite their ecological advantages.

Usage barriers are erected in the kitchen as well as the garage. Several years ago, food companies tried to introduce dry soups in the United States. Although dry soups sold extremely well in Europe, they failed in this country. The main reason: Dry soups required significant changes for the consumer used to condensed soups with all the ingredients packaged and processed in the can. With condensed soups, all the consumer had to do was add water or milk, and the soup was ready in less than five minutes. Dry soups, on the other hand, required adding other ingredients, for which there were no recipes; spending more time preparing them; and being a creative and expert cook. The operational change was so significant that dry soups never took off—until Lipton came out with instant soups that had all the ingredients and only required the consumer to add water!

The same problem faces tofu today. Although tofu is an excellent source of protein, very inexpensive, and highly versatile, it is also tasteless and slimy. Tofu must be blended with other ingredients to add flavor and texture. This process requires cooking skills that are unfortunately becoming obsolete with changing life-styles. It is not even enough to offer potential consumers tofu recipes. At best, tofu will be a great hobby food, to be prepared occasionally. If it is to be sold as a daily staple, it will have to be packaged and processed as a ready-to-eat food or beverage. In fact, some of the recent success of tofu comes from new types of frozen desserts, which are based on tofu rather than cream or yogurt.

Solutions

Solutions to usage barrier problems are discovered by field testing the innovation to observe how it fits into the customer's operational routine. This is a very common procedure followed in experiments with carpooling, videotex, and many social programs. Innovators must learn by trial and error because it is impossible to anticipate all the problems the customers are likely to experience as they use the new product or service. The underlying principle is customer understanding *prior* to the design and market introduction of the innovation. With the needs, habits, and fears of the customer in mind, one can try the systems approach, the integration strategy, or, if all else fails, force.

Systems. The first and probably the most overlooked solution is to develop a systems perspective. After all, any new product or service interacts with other products used by and activities performed by the customer. If an innovating firm looks at the whole operation, it can estimate much better whether its new offering will fit into the existing system. Dishwashers, for example, did not fit into existing kitchen systems until home builders began to include them in the design of new kitchens. This also seems to be a problem for trash compactors. Unless they are prebuilt in new or remodeled kitchens, they are unlikely to be accepted.

The extraordinary success of minivans can be directly attributed to this systems perspective. Most vans were designed for commercial use and could not be parked in the standard home garage. Chrysler Corporation redesigned the van so that it would fit into existing garages and thus into the driving usage system of the average consumer. The rest is history!

Integration. A related solution to customer usage resistance is to integrate the innovation into the precedent activity or product. In other words, rather than selling the product or service to

Practical Objections

the end users, it must be sold to someone else as an original equipment supplier. For example, many peripheral manufacturers decided to sell their printers to IBM, Digital, and Honeywell so that they would be integrated into the computer systems with no compatibility problems. Similarly, cellular mobile telephone manufacturers have recently begun selling the car telephones to car makers so they can be factory-installed just as radios, air conditioners, and other accessories are.

Force. Finally, it is sometimes possible to overcome usage barriers by making the innovation mandatory through government legislation. This is, of course, a very risky strategy and can only be used in situations where it is clear to lawmakers that the customers/voters will benefit from the innovation. The strategy has been successfully employed by the producers of smoke detectors, seat belts, and lead free gasoline.

The Value Barrier

A second functional and very important category of customer resistance has to do with value. In this instance, value is a quantifiable measure equal to the performance–price ratio of the innovation as compared to existing alternatives. Unless the innovation either offers a strong performance and/or a strong price value to the customers, there is no incentive for them to change their buying habits. Unfortunately, most new products and services tend to be either "me, too" imitations or else inferior to existing alternatives. Why should customers choose something new that is inferior to or, at best, on a par with their present choices? Incredibly, corporations often do not understand this simple logic and proceed to the marketplace with innovations that only offer trade-offs for the customer, not clearly superior choices. When the long distance business was deregulated, for instance, many new entrants offered a strong price discount, which motivated some customers to switch to the new firms. As the price gap narrowed between AT&T and these other common carriers, however, the incentive for customers to switch from AT&T disappeared.

In contrast, the Japanese tend to offer not only a strong price value, but also a definable performance value. Their products, from consumer electronics to automobiles, are not only priced competitively, but seem to have qualities and features that customers want and need.

The long distance phone service case is, unfortunately, more common than the Japanese model. Consider the story of automatic teller machines (ATMs). Compared to the existing options available to the customer, ATMs offer neither performance value nor price value. They are restricted in the types of transactions available to customers. They cannot, for example, open a new account, issue an overseas draft, loan money, or perform any of a number of services that are routinely the province of human personnel. Their only advantage is time and place convenience. ATMs are usually available 24 hours a day and in locations such as shopping malls and supermarkets that are more convenient to the customer. They are, in short, an inferior alternative to existing banking operations purely on practical grounds—not even considering people's preference for dealing with humans rather than machines.

Similarly, there is no price difference between regular banking and ATM banking. The customer pays the same price, whether using regular tellers or ATMs.

Why would anyone like to do business with a machine unless he or she hates people? It would appear that the best way for ATMs to provide extra value and thus be commercially effective is not to function as a replacement of the human teller but as an added benefit to the customer in places and at times when customers do not have access to the human tellers. Therefore, ATMs should be distributed wherever nonbank transactions take place: retail stores, supermarkets, gasoline stations, post offices, and so on. The procedure would be very similar to how bank cards are used. Furthermore, machines ought to be positioned in the bank as a backup device. If the customer has a simple transaction, such as cash vending, he or she can go to either the teller or the ATM. The more complex transactions should be separated and offered on a dedicated basis through the human teller. This concept is similar to the check-in procedures at the airline ticket counters. The customer can check his or her baggage at curbside and go to the gate, check in through the agent if he or she has a ticket with proper reservations, or purchase the ticket at the counter and check in the luggage.

We have seen a number of gadgets invented or designed with no apparent thought given to providing customer utility above and beyond the existing product. The famous vegematic, the electric toothbrush, the electric knife, and even the electric spoon quickly come to mind. Most of them either die right away or degenerate into fads or novelty items.

Perhaps a more significant innovation in recent years has been the video disc player. RCA invested more than $600 million in this technology and touted it as the next major revolution in consumer electronics. Unfortunately, from the customer perspective, it was inferior in value compared to the emerging VCR alternative. First of all, the video disc could play, but not record. If one considers that video tape is only an extension of audio tape, it should be easy to recognize that consumers would prefer being able to play *and* record rather than simply play. Second, the video disc required purchase of discs that could not be used for anything else. Video cassettes, on the other hand, can be reused for different purposes. Third, the programming for disc players was restricted to only what the disc producers could offer, thus further limiting its potential. Despite all this, the video disc could still have succeeded if it had been positioned for very high quality, serious programming, similar to how hi-fi stereos competed when audio tape recorders came into the marketplace. But RCA did not adopt this strategy. Once the Japanese VCR producers began to drop their prices, the disc player had no price value, either, and the customer barriers were way too high to overcome.

Another illuminating case of value barriers hindering the adoption of innovative products has to do with a form of office automation. Earlier, we discussed the corporate operational barriers that confronted the new video teleconferencing technology. To make matters worse, those companies and organizations that have already installed the equipment to provide the capacity for video teleconferencing are finding out that the utilization rate is so low and network capacity is so high that the performance–price value has fallen below that of existing alternatives. Perhaps the only benefit still available occurs when the top officer of the corporation must simultaneously communicate a message to several locations. These instances—announcements about mergers, acquisitions, or bankruptcies; or reaching stockholders at remote locations for the annual shareholder meeting—are not frequent, however. In other words, video teleconferencing probably has value in communications from one to many points and in one-way communications similar to network television programs. As a two-way interactive system in a many-to-many configuration, it is still not cost effective in relation to audio teleconferencing.

A second area of office automation meeting customer-value resistance relates to personal computers. As we discussed earlier, although the PC has many features and functions, most corporate customers limit their use to relatively simple word processing activities. Therefore, the value of the PC relative to alternatives such as word processing units is low—one reason why the PC revolution has been considerably slower than forecasted. Of course, as PC prices comes down and as IBM clones start entering the market, we should expect the more versatile PCs to take over the typewriter business from word processors. Until then, neither the performance value nor price value seems to be in favor of the PC.

Another pertinent story comes from a completely different industrial sector. Several years ago, DuPont produced a rev-

Practical Objections

olutionary substitute for leather called Corfam. It had all the properties of leather, especially breathability. It felt like leather and could be offered in more variety than leather. DuPont conducted extensive research in an attempt to discover whether consumers would resist the innovation because of tradition or image problems. Their findings were encouraging. The consumer research clearly suggested that Corfam would be an excellent leather substitute with market potential comparable to nylon and polyester, which had successfully replaced silk, cotton, and other natural fibers.

Unfortunately, Corfam turned out to be a failure. It appears the price value of Corfam relative to leather was not as good as, for example, nylon's to silk. Leather is abundant on a worldwide basis. Countries like Brazil and India have vast capacities for producing leather, and it is extraordinarily cheap compared to U.S. domestic leather. Also, shoe manufacturers had to significantly alter their manufacturing facilities to accommodate Corfam. Since Corfam provided neither a price value nor a performance value, it was natural that shoe manufacturers would be reluctant to invest in new plants and machinery to accommodate Corfam: the savings in raw material was not big enough to justify capitalization. To make matters worse, shoe manufacturing moved overseas, and countries like Italy, Brazil, and India began to manufacture shoes with significant labor cost advantages.

Another very clever idea, this time in agriculture, also failed because of a value perception problem; but this story has a happier ending for one of the parties concerned. Some entrepreneur designed contact lenses for chickens! The purpose was to distort their vision to reduce cannibalism, which is common in a chicken coop as chickens establish their pecking hierarchy. The current preventive procedure is to debeak the chickens when they are young. However, even beakless chickens manage to kill about 10 percent of their number.

Unfortunately, it appeared that if the contact lenses were kept in the eyes of the chicken for one full year (the normal cycle for egg laying), they actually blinded the chickens because they would not allow the corneas to breathe. It seems that a blind chicken is more vicious than a normal chicken. A coop of blind chickens would actually have a *higher* cannibalism rate. Second, the cost of the contact lenses per chicken was higher than debeaking. Since the farmer could not get any additional value (feed savings, mortality drop, etc.), there was no reason to switch to the new technology. However, as promised, the story has a happy ending, at least for the chicken farmer. It turns out that it was not the vision distortion but the red color of the lens that quieted down the chickens. Therefore, there was an easier and a lot cheaper solution: put red light bulbs in the chicken coops!

In the consumer goods area, vast numbers of product innovations in foods, drugs, and cosmetics turn out to be failures for one simple reason: Very few of them offer either performance or price value over the existing alternatives. Ironically, the packaged goods industry, which does probably the most research on customers, has one of the highest new product failure rates. Most of these, to repeat, are due to lack of value: Most are simply "me, too" brand names hoping to capture customer demand by some clever advertising or promotion scheme. It is, therefore, not surprising that pioneer brand names such as Tide (detergents), Colgate (toothpaste), Coca-Cola (soft drinks), Tylenol (aspirin substitute), Bayer (aspirin), Mennen (after-shave), L'Oreal (hair coloring), Gillette (razor blades), and so on continue to dominate the industry.

Only when a true value is created by the innovation, either in superior performance or significant cost savings, is it likely that the new product will succeed in the mass market. This truth applies to services as well. McDonald's (fast food), Sears (automotive repair), American Express (traveler's checks and travel cards), and other established businesses are safe from attack if the challenging innovation does not offer *greater* value.

Practical Objections 77

Solutions

All solutions are not as simple nor as elegant as putting red lights in chicken coops. They are, however, possible. The key is to provide *relative* value. Innovations must offer greater performance or a better price or be positioned against a different competitor.

Performance. The first strategy for overcoming the value barrier is to provide significant performance value over existing alternatives. For example, electronic calculators performed engineering functions and financial calculations that the old electromechanical calculators could not. They were also more portable and could be used as alarm clocks. Similarly, microwave ovens added significant performance capabilities over the electric range, including portability and electronic controls. Finally, many new telephone sets have features such as redial and memory buttons that were simply not possible with basic telephones.

Price. A second solution is to reduce the manufacturing costs and pass on the savings to the customers. Timex was able to reduce production costs on their watches several years ago by switching to pin lever movement. In the process, they literally created the mass market for watches. More recently, Japanese watchmakers such as Seiko, Casio, and Citizen have continued to generate significant cost savings by improving styling so as to eliminate materials and parts and by increasing reliability. Finally, price reductions through cost savings constitutes the major thrust in the minicomputer industry. Within less than a decade, the big minicomputers produced by Digital, Prime, and Data General all have been reduced to desk-top models, with more features and functions and better reliability, at half the cost of the older-generation machines.

Positioning. A third strategy attempts to add value by product positioning. This approach is more difficult to implement and requires greater subtlety. The innovator must analyze all existing substitutes across a very broad spectrum and position the new product in a niche or application where it has a strong performance–price superiority over its alternatives. There are many examples, but the best involves a very familiar product: canned soup.

Campbell's positioning move is motivated by some of the demographic shifts discussed in chapter 1. For years, Campbell's was entrenched as the companion to the sandwich for children's lunch at home. Today, the trends toward single-person households and dual-income families have sharply reduced the number of times kids get lunch from mom. In addition, new life-styles reduce the regularity of home-cooked meals.

As a result, Campbell's is positioning soup as an easy-to-fix, inexpensive, familiar item for an adult's main meal and emphasizing its nutritional quality ("soup is good food"; "chunky" soups also "eat like a meal"). Soup from Campbell's is thus competitive in price and performance (taste, nutrition, convenience) in a new market segment, namely the main meal at dinnertime. It is perceived as the best value when compared to frozen dinners, eating at a restaurant, or preparing a full dinner at home.

The Risk Barrier

A third major customer barrier is related to risk. It arises because all innovations, to some extent, represent uncertainty and pose potential side effects that cannot be anticipated completely. Customers know there are risks and try to postpone adopting an innovation until they can learn more about it.

Several types of risks are inherent in an innovation; some are very hard and quantifiable, some are more elusive and subjective. Perhaps the most obvious is the economic risk. If the innovation fails to gain mass acceptance, or if it is a first-generation product that will be improved later, the customer

Practical Objections

perceives that the financial investment in the new product, service, or process could easily be lost. The higher the cost, as with capital goods, the higher the perceived economic risk.

The second type of risk is physical: harm to person or property that may be inherent in the innovation. Because they are designed to act on the body, new drugs commonly carry some physical risk. Farmers are unwilling to experiment with new insecticides, fertilizers, and herbicides because of the fear of permanent soil damage. Consumers worry that new hair spray and hair colors will permanently bleach out their hair.

A third type of risk is performance uncertainty. The customer worries that the technology may not be as yet fully tested and tried and, therefore, that the product or service may not function properly and reliably. New cars are famous for generating uncertainty; that is why auto companies offer extensive warranties — and why no one really feels comfortable with a new car until it has been driven for a while and all the bugs worked out.

As always, we will illustrate the various types of risk barriers with examples from different industries. The first is physical risk. In an earlier section, we discussed the regulatory barriers to the innovative process of food preservation known as irradiation. There is also a significant physical risk factor at work here because the average citizen is very much concerned about radiation. Recent nuclear energy accidents at Three Mile Island and Chernobyl have increased the public's concern about nuclear technologies. This concern is easily manifested in anything having to do with food. Most consumers are afraid that if food is treated with low-level radiation, it is likely to have long-term consequences such as cancer. Even though scientific evidence suggests that low-level radiation energy may be less harmful than the chemical preservatives found in foods and agricultural products, the association of risk with radiation is simply too high for the public to accept this technology.

A similar concern is raised about sugar substitutes,

whether saccharine, cyclamate, or the more recent NutraSweet (Aspartame). In fact, the overall public confidence in processed foods and drugs has fallen to such a low level that we are concerned about practically everything we eat today, despite a continuous rise in life expectancy and substantial evidence that we are more healthy today than at any time in history.

The best examples of customer resistance due to perceived economic risk are personal computers and video cameras. Many interested consumers are postponing their purchases because they believe, quite correctly, that if they wait, a much better product with a lower price tag will be on the market in the next few months. They learned from the VCR experience. They can see it happening with such well-known personal computers as IBM, Apple, and Tandy, and with various brands of video cameras. Ironically, the economic risk is created by economics: The sharp experience curves and economy of scale of the consumer electronics industry improves products and reduces prices.

This same risk-avoidance tendency is equally prevalent in the corporate world. For example, many companies decide to wait to upgrade their computer systems in anticipation of a new generation of IBM products with a better price–performance ratio. In fact, several IBM competitors have charged that IBM deliberately announces that it will introduce a new generation of mainframe systems to influence data processing managers to avoid switching to competitors with superior products or systems.

Performance uncertainty commonly creates risk-aversion barriers in the area of international trade. Even though it is possible to procure cheaper components from offshore manufacturers, many automobile and appliance companies avoid buying new components and parts from these sources because they fear product failure. If the component or part fails, they will be unable to maintain delivery schedules and provide on-site main-

Practical Objections

tenance services. Economic risks surface here as well, because customers worry about the consequences of part failure and product liability. The fear had a real basis for the garment industry several years ago when they relied on Indian textiles, especially bleeding madras. The delivery schedules were not maintained, the window for the fashion season closed on them, and all parties lost millions of dollars in missed sales opportunities.

But risk barriers are perhaps strongest in the services sector, second only to foods. Most services are labor intensive and, therefore, possess greater variance in performance and reliability. It is not easy to deliver as promised in a labor-intensive service, and the customer knows the risks. That is perhaps why more than 75 percent of all phone service customers have decided to stay with AT&T long distance service even though a number of competitors offered their service on an equal access basis. Part of the reason, of course, is the competitors' lack of experience. Most are new entrants in the business and perhaps do not possess AT&T's level of expertise, especially in support services such as billing and operator assistance. One would expect that if the divested Bell Operating Companies or well known vendors such as IBM had offered the services, more customers would have exercised their options and switched.

The herd mentality is also strong in the health care field, even among highly educated people. Most doctors do not adopt new drugs or medical practices until they are fully tested, certified, and widely used. Newness increases the fear of malpractice suits; the thought of legal action leads to depressing thoughts of high insurance premiums. Old becomes safer, even if less effective medically. A recent technology for cancer detection, thermography, is now considered far safer, very cost-effective, and as reliable as any other procedure, but most U.S. doctors were reluctant to adopt it because it was not widely used in the American medical community. (Happily, thermography is now gaining acceptance; see chapter 7.)

Solutions

You knock down risk barriers by striking at the source of the fear. Risk, or the perception of risk, can be minimized with free trials, testimonials, and system packaging.

Free Trials. The most common practical method of overcoming the risk barrier has been to offer the new technology, product, or service on a trial basis and with complete guarantees and reassurances. Trialability of the new technology is the key. For example, when American farmers did not believe in the 2,4-D preweed killer and worried about the chemical's effects on the crop, the manufacturer offered farmers a free trial on a 5- to 10-acre field right next to the farmer's other acreage in which the same crop was grown with more traditional methods.

Although trialability is often a good solution, it is not applicable to all cases. There are situations in which a customer cannot try out a product on a limited basis with only a limited negative effect. For example, new surgical procedures for such vital organs as the heart, the kidneys, and the eyes can cause irreparable damage if something goes wrong. Similarly, when a company decides to computerize, it is often an irreversible decision. It simply has to be careful and protect the downside risk. IBM is reputed to capitalize on this risk aversion by promising excellent support and hand holding in case something goes wrong. The IBM version is, in fact, a strategic variation that does more than minimize risk; it obliterates risk.

Testimonials. A second method for dampening the fears of risk is to elicit endorsements and testimonials. This approach is common in the introduction of new movies, new restaurants, and new books. In fact, we obtained good testimonials for this book from well respected practitioners and academics in order to minimize the risk (economic and uncertain performance, but not physical) that might discourage potential readers. Of course, testimonials must come from experts; and, of course, they must

Practical Objections 83

objectively evaluate the innovation before endorsing it. The customer is simply too smart and too cynical to believe that all endorsements are genuine and based on objective criteria. Nonetheless, testimonials and endorsements do work for most products and services. We have found them effectively used for such diverse products as pharmaceuticals, machine tools, appliances, and automobiles and for services offered by brokerage, insurance, accounting, and legal firms.

System Packaging. The final mode of attack on risk barriers entails introducing the innovation as a component in a system so that the end user does not or cannot evaluate it independently. In other words, the new product or service should be offered to an original equipment manufacturer (OEM) whose reputation and reliability will be used to offset the perception of risk associated with the new product or service. The OEM or reseller becomes the customer instead of the end user. Michelin successfully introduced radial tires in the U.S. by selling them under the Sears label. That is, they sold their tires to Sears, and Sears' reputation sold the tires to consumers as part of their auto service packaging. Many professional services, such as plumbing, heating, cooling, fencing, remodeling, roofing, and others, are today offered by independent contractors but under the Sears name, with the Sears reputation and guarantee.

Similarly, imitation cheese is consumed by the public without the public's knowledge. Imitation cheese—real food, but not a dairy product—is mostly sold to fast food chains, which then offer it as an ingredient in their cheeseburgers. Variations on this strategy are everywhere. Most new drugs are prescribed by the hospital, where neither the intern nor the patient has any choice. Offshore manufacturers of garments, consumer electronics, and even office equipment all offer their products through well known corporations, like Arrow Shirts, General Electric, and Savin, with reputations that mitigate the risk of purchase.

System packaging, of course, presupposes that the innovation is good and has no known side effects. This last strategy will, in fact, boomerang if the new product or service is not reliable.

PSYCHOLOGICAL BLOCKS

The Tradition Barrier

The first major psychological source of customer resistance comes from the cultural change necessitated by the innovation. Cultural discontinuity is as much a problem in the corporate world as it is in the consumer world. Corporate norms, corporate cultures, and corporate values are counterparts to social norms and social and family values. An innovation is resisted when it requires making changes in the traditions established by the corporate or societal culture; the greater the change, the greater the resistance.

As the U.S. economy becomes more and more service-oriented, we see more evidence of customers erecting cultural or tradition-based barriers to the increasing number of innovative services. It is, for example, still socially unacceptable to use computerized dating or to advertise in the newspaper for a potential spouse. Even singles bars as meeting places carry a social stigma. In a somewhat analogous professional situation, most women executives find traveling difficult because of social connotations associated with eating alone in a restaurant or sleeping alone in a hotel room. Similar social concerns are associated with coed health spas and bathroom facilities in the corporate world of country clubs and athletic clubs. Finally, the health care field is encountering a lot of tradition-based resistance to such practices as the use of surrogate mothers, the adoption of interracial children, organ transplants, and other socially integrative medical practices.

In the computer world, corporate culture and tradition was a major barrier when IBM tried to introduce the concept of word processing centers to the office, because that required executives to give up their personal secretaries. The secretaries would be housed in a word processing center where they would work more with machines than with human beings. The status of both the executives and the secretaries was being lowered in the process. In fact, the informal power of the secretary through confidential knowledge as well as control of the executive calendar was threatened by the new technology. In short, the word processing centers were a threat to the existing organizational structure.

IBM was, however, successful in diffusing the resistance to the new order in those situations where the corporation already had a stenopool. "Upgrading" a stenopool to a word processing center created very little tradition-based resistance. At the higher levels of management, IBM and other innovative computer firms such as Savin, Wang, and Xerox introduced word processing in the form of stand-alone units that replaced the traditional typewriters but kept everything else intact.

Similar tradition-based resistance is very prevalent among blue-collar workers when corporations attempt to introduce new work procedures, such as quality circles, physical exercises before the shift, or automated processes. In fact, it often requires union blessing and union persuasion to change the factory tradition. In this case, line managers, foremen, and laborers are the customers for the innovation. Their natural human inclination is to resist changes in their traditional roles.

Tradition also plays a significant role in industrial supplies such as packaging materials. For example, glass is still considered socially more elegant than plastic. Therefore, most socially conspicuous-consumption products, such as formal dinnerware, decorations, and packaging of certain foods and beverages, is dominated by glass, even though glass is more costly and more hazardous. And the same barriers are erected against the substitution of plastic for metal in very basic appliances. A plastic washing machine tub, for example, is considered by consumers to be inferior to a steel tub. A plastic refrigerator, even though it may provide more color, style, and other aesthetic utility, is considered socially inferior to a metal refrigerator. Finally, plastic flowers and plants are more cost effective and easier to maintain in offices and homes, but there is social stigma attached to artificial objects.

Fortunately, over time, technological innovations do succeed and replace more expensive and primitive but natural resources and materials. The process requires long cycles of market development, however, because it takes a long time for customers to break their traditions and switch to a new technology. Today, we see plastic materials in televisions and stereos, in food and beverage packaging, in home construction materials, and even in hospital linens and garments!

We are perhaps more tradition bound in our eating habits than in any other type of consumption. Therefore, innovative uses of foods and beverages or the introduction of foods new to the subculture have been thwarted by tradition barriers more often than most other products. For example, we still think of cranberry sauce as a Thanksgiving relish. This tradition has made it very difficult for Ocean Spray to promote its use for other occasions. Similarly, many years ago, homemakers were resistant to instant coffee because they believed family members and friends would look down on them as lazy, unloving spendthrifts. Until recently, most Americans were reluctant to experiment beyond the basic meat-and-potato meal. In northern Europe even today, eating pasta, spaghetti, and pizza is considered anticultural and socially rebellious. New food products such as yogurt and tofu were complete social outcasts until recently. Drinking beer was considered blue collar, and gin and tonic was a sissy drink that no real man would prefer over a shot of whiskey. The examples go on and on. Attitudes can change over time, but until they do, the barriers are up.

The problem is not confined to industrialized nations. Tradition continuity is probably the biggest obstacle to product innovation in many Third World countries. Religion and past

Psychological Blocks

local traditions discourage consumers from accepting modern foods, clothing, and life-styles in general. Successful products in one culture fail in another in incredible numbers because they cannot penetrate the barriers of tradition. The best examples come from the drug industry. Many traditional societies, such as China and India, have always relied on herbal remedies, home remedies, and such mechanical procedures as acupuncture and acupressure to treat disease. They therefore resist using Western over-the-counter drugs, even such basic products as aspirin and antihistamines.

Solutions

We've already mentioned that time erodes traditional barriers. Besides the virtue of patience, marketers of innovative products need to cultivate the basic values of respect, understanding, and education. Traditions can be changed if approached with the proper attitude.

Understanding and Respect. One must first understand and respect cultural traditions. It is surprising how many foreign product or service failures can be attributed to ignorance of and arrogance about other cultures. For example, several attempts have been made to establish the beef industry in India without success. Traditional respect for the cow will simply not permit slaughterhouses, let alone hamburger diets, in the subcontinent. These same destructive attitudes are in force even within the United States when companies try to market certain products or services to ethnic subcultures. It is important for the corporation to educate its managers, engineers, and executives about the nature and tenacity of cultural traditions.

Furthermore, even trying to change mainstream cultural traditions can evoke strong negative feelings against the corporation. Citicorp learned that lesson recently when it tried to change the banking habits of its individual depositors. The bank insisted that unless a person had a $2,500 minimum balance in his or her account, he or she would have to use the automatic teller machines. The human tellers were to be limited to the bank's better customers. This innovative procedure would have worked if it were not for the fact that people had been conditioned to interact with human tellers; they were very uncomfortable with an alternate system, no matter how efficient. After a short experiment, Citicorp was forced to reverse the policy.

More recently, United Airlines announced that only full-fare passengers could reserve seat assignments in advance. The policy immediately generated a strong protest from the many corporate travelers who were using low fares and thus were denied advanced seating. Once again, traditional prerogatives were lost, and a new procedure had to be abandoned. United Airlines rescinded the decision within one month.

Innovative promotions, products, and distribution concepts have often met with strong resistance in foreign countries. This resistance was generated because corporations simply did not attempt to understand even basic cultural differences. How else can we explain failures of bed manufacturers in Japan, or cake mix manufacturers in England, or mouthwash manufacturers in Asia?

The second of those cases is particularly instructive. Betty Crocker could not sell U.S.-style moist, rich dessert cakes in England because the British tradition is to eat drier cakes, cookies, and biscuits by hand at tea time. The U.S. product did not fit British preferences and so failed to gain acceptance.

Education. A second strategy for overcoming the barriers of customer tradition involves market education. In foreign countries especially, this is a very slow process and often requires government encouragement and support. This approach has been successful in the health care area. For example, international organizations such as the World Health Organization (WHO) have literally eradicated several dreaded diseases such as smallpox and yellow fever in many countries through education. They have taught people the basic preventive procedures of early inoculation, proper sanitary practices, and the use of modern chemicals. Similarly, successful efforts in birth control in countries like Singapore, India, and China have been achieved through massive educational efforts.

Massive education has been used effectively in more developed countries as well. The acceptance of modern farming mehods in this century has been accomplished by a concerted and organized educational effort from university and goverment extension agents. Mass education is currently being employed to promote computer literacy in the United States. Some time ago, national education programs were very successful in teaching us how to conserve energy and in convincing us that the effort was necessary.

Change Agents. The third strategy in combating tradition barriers to innovation is the use of change agents. This approach is often referred to as the opinion leadership or leading edge strategy. It involves the cooperation of the society's change agents to endorse the innovation and to actually become the first users. For example, in both farming and medicine, the most successful adoptions of innovative products and/or services were first targeted to highly respected industry leaders. In farming, that means first approaching university agriculture extension people, the United States Department of Agriculture (USDA), and the highly respected big farmers who are receptive to modern farm practices. In medicine, innovators look to highly respected hospitals, clinics, and physicians who have reputations for leadership. IBM has consistently used the leading edge—business customers in each industry group such as banks, education, brokerage, and insurance—to embrace new technologies. In fact, the leadership strategy is a favorite in the office equipment and office automation field, and it is practiced by major suppliers such as Xerox, Wang, and AT&T.

In some countries, it is common to use the famous trickle-down theory in the change agent process: The elite of the society adopts an innovation, which is then adopted by the masses. Similarly, most innovations are first introduced in metropolitan areas, where education and income levels tend to be high. Urban users then act as change agents for the rural markets.

In the United States, there is overwhelming evidence that the emerging change agents or the leading edge customers for consumer products are the well educated young white-collar professionals, commonly referred to as yuppies (young urban professionals) or their variations, such as buppies (black urban professionals), or huppies (Hispanic urban professionals). Yuppies, buppies, and huppies are especially influential in the introduction of innovations in consumer electronics, automobiles, and personal computers; high-tech services such as videotex and computerized banking; as well as life-style activities pertaining to new foods, drinks, and restaurants. In the United States, you can sometimes change traditions quickly by selling innovations to the "_uppies."

The Image Barrier

The final area of customer resistance has to do with image. Innovations acquire a certain identity at inception solely from their origins: product class, industry, and country. If these associations are unfavorable as a result of stereotyped thinking, they create barriers to adoption. Image is by definition more perceptual than real. While we all know that people stereotype consumer products, we are discovering that stereotyping is universal and cuts across both industrial and consumer markets.

For example, many people believe that the U.S. postal system is really bad. It is, however, one of the most efficient in the world. The same misconception holds for all regulated industries: water, gas, electricity, telephones—probably because of our belief that monopoly is always bad and competition

Psychological Blocks

good. Other common stereotypes are also false. In fact, small businesses are *not* more entrepreneurial than large businesses; decentralized corporations are *not* more efficient than centralized corporations; private universities are *not* more innovative than state universities; private schools do *not* necessarily provide better education than public schools. The list could go on and on.

In addition to calcified thought, image barriers are built from violated social taboos, from stigmas associated with new technologies, or from deep-seated psychological forces that may be aroused by the innovation.

One of the best examples of poor image from association with origins is the one that adhered at one time to machine tools made in India. India was and is one of the largest producers of industrial machine tools such as lathes, milling machines, and grinding machines. Until recently, however, India suffered from a negative image that had nothing to do with the quality of its industrial products. Most machine tool buyers in the advanced countries simply did not believe that what they thought of as a country of snake charmers and roaming cows could ever produce any kind of machine tool, let alone good quality tools. Furthermore, the geocultural distance between India and Western Europe hurt business negotiations and also restricted after-sales support services, which are extremely important in the machine tools industry. Indian firms put forth a lot of educational effort, established showrooms in various European cities, and aligned with highly reputed distributors, before Western European customers would even consider buying from them.

The negative image of the country is also a barrier for many other Third World nations, including Korea, Taiwan, and Brazil. In contrast, Japan and Germany have very positive images regarding the quality of their products and services. They need not, therefore, contend with initial skepticism when they introduce their new products to the business world. It is unfortunate that the excellent reputation of U.S. made products and services has been on the decline in recent years—both overseas and within the U.S. market. We can thus expect image barriers to begin impeding the introduction of innovations from U.S. firms.

Not all unpleasant associations have something to do with the country of origin, of course. Several years ago, a University of Illinois professor produced specialty chemicals that could convert cow's dung into animal feed. It was a very cost-effective process and could have saved considerable sums for big feedlot operators because the average cow leaves undigested significant amounts of energy and nutrients from its normal feed, which can be recovered and recycled by treating the manure. Unfortunately, the image of feeding cows with their own manure was so negative that feedlot operators, their health experts, and even governmental agencies were skeptical or reluctant to endorse the idea. Since most cattle are actually owned by investors, the feedlot operators even worried about negative publicity associated with recycling manure as animal feed. The image problem was so formidable that the innovation had to be abandoned.

The history of an innovative means of transportation, the motorcycle, has a happier conclusion. In the 1950s, the motorcycle did not seem to have much of a commercial future because it was associated with beatniks and gangs. The negative image of the motorcycle in the United States was in sharp contrast to the rest of the world, where it was used for daily transportation to work and sometimes even as a family vehicle for Sunday outings. The college student who could not afford a car was a prime target for the motorcycle, if the negative image could be changed. It took redesign and unique advertising by Honda to turn the trick, and motorcycles became legitimate recreational or transportation vehicles.

Most professional services also suffer from less-than-ideal stereotyping, some almost as severe as motorcycles. For exam-

Psychological Blocks

ple, consultants are often equated with prostitutes, or they are labeled as hit-and-run suppliers. Lawyers are referred to as ambulance chasers, medical doctors are called butchers, and professors are considered eggheads who live in ivory towers. In fact, every occupation has some image difficulties. Consequently, innovative products and services related to those occupations must, just because of the association, create a measure of customer resistance.

But not even a professor who is also a consultant and a lawyer has the worst image problem. The worst image belongs to a common fruit—the prune. The very mention of the word *prune* starts to generate nervous laughter. The average person will avoid admitting to a liking for or even a need to eat prunes. Whether it is the laxative property of the prunes or the unconscious association of prunes with wrinkles and old age, somehow they have become the shunned fruit. Therefore, any product innovation related to prunes is likely to be resisted by consumers. Do not expect to see prune juice cocktail or prune bran flakes any time soon, unless they are positioned as medicinal or essential.

Foods probably have the most stereotypes. We have images conjured up by soul food, pasta, Mexican food, Indian curry, Japanese sushi, and Chinese rice. We also have negative images about liver and kidneys. Foods tend to have strong traditions and strong image associations that create barriers to innovative uses, such as ethnic foods sold in nonethnic markets and specialty foods served on a more general basis.

Solutions

One of the great discoveries of the twentieth century has been that images can be consciously altered, even completely fabricated. A corollary discovery that we seem less inclined to accept is that a phony image will eventually be discovered and will be turned on its creator.

Invent an Image. The first strategy and probably the most successful is to make fun of the image and of how silly it is for people to carry such stereotypes. The prune growers association has tried this approach several times. For example, they hired Stan Freeburg, who came out with such classic slogans as "Today the pits, tomorrow the wrinkles" in promoting the pitless prunes.

Goldstar, Korea's multibillion-dollar consumer electronics company, is making fun of people's negative image of Korean products in their attempt to sell televisions, VCRs, and microwaves. Honda countered the beatnik image of motorcycles with a campaign that showed such respectable people as a priest or a little old lady riding on a Honda with a caption: "The nicest people ride on a Honda."

Create an Image. The second strategy is to create a unique image for the product or service. For example, in order to negate its then current image of being a woman's brand (because of the filter with the red tip), Marlboro cigarettes created the unique cowboy image for itself. Similarly, to combat the negative image of light beer, Miller beer used lots of retired athletes and tough guys to sell its product. Finally, to combat the weak image of wine coolers, associated with low alcohol content, Gallo wines created a unique position with actors portraying Frank Bartles and Ed James as folksy winemakers.

Borrow an Image. The third solution to the image barrier problem is to consciously associate the new product or service with something or someone having an established positive public image. The range of this strategy is astounding. It can pair celebrities with warnings about dreaded diseases (Rock Hudson with AIDS, athletes and actors with cocaine), Indian machine tools with reputable local distributors, compatible software with IBM, and so on.

SUMMARY

Customer resistance to innovation can be very intense because innovation disrupts people's lives; it can also be hard to control because customers are outside the corporate structure. Companies that understand these problems, however, can still bring their innovations to market without fatal distress. Customer barriers concerning usage patterns, economic values, and risks are primarily functional problems; those having to do with tradition and image are essentially psychological.

Usage barriers are erected when an innovation is not compatible with the customer's existing workflows, practices, or habits. Examples range from computers and teleconferencing to carpools and tofu. Firms can sometimes market the innovation by selling it as part of a system or by integrating it into a preceding activity or product. Customers erect value barriers when they perceive a poor performance–price ratio, as with automatic teller machines and contact lenses for chickens. Innovative products will only succeed if they provide superior *relative* value in performance and/or price against the alternatives. Risk barriers are built from concerns about economic loss or physical harm or from product uncertainty. Innovating firms can respond by offering free trials, soliciting testimonials, and packaging within an accepted system.

Tradition-based resistance is created when social norms or the values of the corporate culture are threatened. IBM's attempt at introducing word processing centers is illustrative. Besides cultivating patience, firms must develop an understanding of and respect for cultural traditions. They can also educate the market and work through change agents. Finally, some innovations face image barriers because of negative association (Indian machine tools) or stereotyped thinking (prunes). Firms can try to create a new image, generate positive associations, and break down calcified thinking with humor.

In chapters 2 and 3 we have defined and illustrated corporate and customer barriers to the marketing of innovations. But understanding and identifying the barriers is not enough; they must be measured before a strategic response can be formulated. That will be the task of chapter 4.

Couretas, J. "Cellular Phone Makers Aim at a Moving Market." *Business Marketing*, July 1984, 45–55.

Donath, B., "Can Your New Product Pass this Test?: How to Score Its Chances with the Sheth New Product Screen." *Business Marketing*, July 1984, 66–68.

McManus, K. "Car Phones that Really Work." *Forbes*, Apr. 23, 1984, 124–125.

Smith, J. "How Processing with Microwave Affects Food Qualities." *Food Product Development*, Feb. 1977, 60.

"Diet Drinks Outpace Field: No Caffeine Segment for Real." *Beverage World*. March 1983, 30–31.

"Yogurt Makers Try a Mass Marketing Recipe." *Business Week*, Nov. 8, 1976, 91–95.

"Choosing a Typewriter Is no Longer a Simple Job." *Business Week*, June 22, 1981, 97–98.

"Microwave: The Next Health Hazard?" *Business Week*, Dec. 25, 1971, 21.

"Pushbutton Can Takes Off on Its Own." *Business Week*, April 11, 1964, 102.

"Testing Time for Tofu." *Food Manufacture*, May 1984, 76–77.

"Soy Products in Foodstuffs." *Food Processing*, Oct. 1983, 45–47.

"Honda's Feature Exterior Plastics." *Plastics World*, Nov. 1983, 9.

"PVC Food Packaging to Grow." *Plastics World*, Nov. 1983, 10.

"Say Cheese: Cemac Food Corp. Keys Expansion to Popularity Boom of Analogs." *Quick Frozen Foods*, Sept. 1981, 36–37.

"Over Microwave Health Hazards." *Telephony*, May 8, 1978, 11–12.

4
Measuring the Barriers

In chapters 2 and 3, we discussed five corporate and five customer barriers that impede innovation. In this chapter, we will focus on one industry—telecommunications—and show how to measure the degree of resistance to innovation adoption created by each of the 10 corporate and customer barriers.

We have chosen only one industry for illustrative purposes to demonstrate that any industry is likely to generate innovations that will encounter both corporate barriers and customer barriers. We have specifically chosen the telecommunications industry for several reasons. First, telecommunications is a universal service that has an impact on everyone. Second, it is going through significant environmental changes, especially technological and regulatory, that are accelerating the process of innovation. The dynamic nature of the industry provides a strong basis for analysis and offers several good current examples and case histories for investigation. Finally, the telecommunications industry is extremely important as a national strategic resource and, therefore, managing the innovation process is crit-

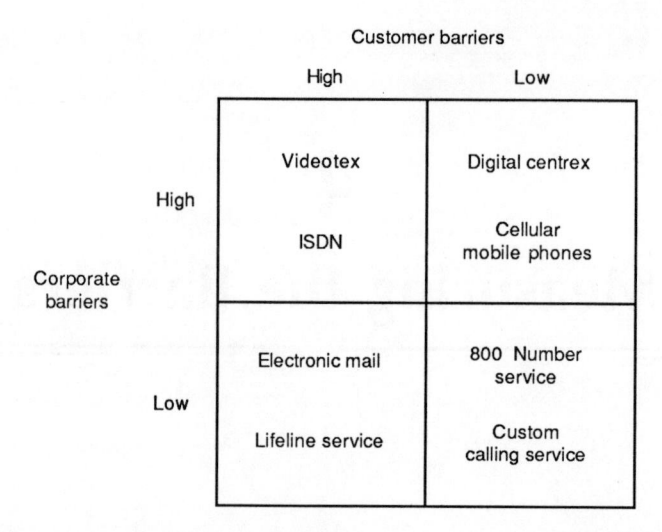

		Customer barriers	
		High	Low
Corporate barriers	High	Videotex ISDN	Digital centrex Cellular mobile phones
	Low	Electronic mail Lifeline service	800 Number service Custom calling service

Figure 4.1. Classification of telecommunications innovations

ical to establishing and maintaining a global competitive advantage.

Figure 4.1 summarizes the specific innovations in telecommunications that will be used to illustrate the measurement procedures. Eight innovations are arranged into four boxes according to the height of the corporate and customer barriers they face. The innovations in the upper-left box, for instance, must overcome both high corporate and high customer barriers. In each box, one innovation is related to the business market and another to the consumer market. We will describe each innovation and then rate the difficulty each faces in overcoming the 10 barriers. We will use the familiar 1 to 10 scale, with 10 indicating the toughest barrier, or the greatest resistance to the acceptance of the innovation in the marketplace.

It might be convenient at this point to review quickly the 10 barriers to innovation. Within the structure of the corporation, innovations are impeded by the following barriers:

1. *Expertise.* Technology-driven innovations and over-specialization

2. *Operations.* Changes required in materials procurement, manufacturing, and worker training
3. *Resources.* Low capital resources and borrowing power
4. *Regulation.* Restrictions from government or within an industry
5. *Market access.* Inability to reach customers because of distribution problems or competitors' strengths

Functional problems and psychological resistance come from customers and form the following barriers:

1. *Usage.* Disruption of existing work flows, practices, and habits
2. *Value.* Low performance–price ratio
3. *Risk.* Waste of money, physical damage, or performance uncertainty
4. *Tradition.* Social norms and cultural attitudes dictating usage
5. *Image.* Taboos, stereotyping, and negative associations

All 10 barriers come into play against the innovative videotex service.

VIDEOTEX

The videotex system consists of a large database of stored information, a digital network, and a terminal in the hands of the users. The terminal is hooked to an existing television set and has a remote keypad with which to input instructions. The terminal is also hooked to the regular telephone line via a modem.

The fundamental characteristic of videotex is that it is interactive. This means that the user can send messages and receive responses. No human voice is involved. The user is essentially talking to a computer that responds intelligently; that is, the computer is programmed to anticipate the user's actions and prompt the user to carry out the next task.

Videotex services are generally offered to the public as a smorgasbord consisting of a menu of services to choose from according to their needs and desires. Videotex can be used to perform business transactions such as commercial banking, electronic shopping, and funds transfer from one account to another. It can also be used for interactive education and learning by allowing people to attend classes at remote locations while sitting at home in front of a television screen. Finally, videotex is an interactive entertainment system that can be used to play electronic games.

Let's evaluate the difficulty of introducing videotex to the market according to its score on first the corporate and then the customer barriers.

Expertise

Videotex requires the integration of at least four areas of technical expertise: database management, intelligent terminals, high-speed interactive networks, and program content. No single company has all these technical capabilities. Therefore, firms have had to form strategic alliances and share each other's expertise. But these technical coalitions have had considerable difficulty putting together a user-friendly system; many companies have abandoned product development. We therefore rate the expertise barrier as very formidable; we give it a score of 8.

Operations

Providers of videotex services must establish separate and dedicated operations for the system in order to offer it to customers. The process is highly specialized, and it is not feasible to integrate it into existing operations, either for information providers or for network operations. Our score of 8 again represents a high barrier to integration with existing operations.

Resources

Since specialized and dedicated efforts are needed for product development, videotex also requires strong financial resources. Indeed, strong supporters of videotex, such as Knight Ridder and AT&T, have pulled out from developing the product and test marketing the technology because of the millions of dollars of commitment that would be needed without any indication of when the payback might begin. Our score of 9 indicates enormous resource allocation, a high barrier to hurdle.

Regulation

Videotex is not a regulated technology (although the Bell local telephone companies are banned from offering it on the regulated side of their business). It has, however, generated considerable public discussion and raised a few regulatory issues. Newspapers are, for instance, worried about the competition for classified ads and the survival, they say, of the free press. This dispute has slowed down full product development. Furthermore, the regulatory climate is, at the least, uncertain, and many suppliers are hesitant to invest in videotex before the regulatory dust settles. Our estimation of the height of the regulatory barrier, where 1 means minimum regulation and 10 means full regulation, is 5.

Market Access

Perhaps the least formidable of corporate barriers to videotex is market access. The distribution channels are in place, except perhaps for billing, installation, and maintenance. Even these could be easily accessed by contractual and/or agency relationships with local telephone companies. Our score here is 2.

The total value of all the structural corporate barriers to videotex is a hefty 32 out of 50. Now let us examine the barriers present on the customer side.

Usage

The biggest customer barrier has been built by usage patterns. Most residential customers have only a single telephone line. If they use the videotex service, they cannot continue normal voice conversation. Recently, Pacific Bell has announced a revolutionary technology (Project Victoria) that splits the single line into multiple channels so that the customer can simultaneously carry on the telephone conversation as well as use the videotex service. However, this potential breakthrough is still at a trial stage and is not available universally.

The user also has to dedicate his television set for videotex when using the service. More importantly, the customer has to buy an intelligent terminal and hook it up to both the television set and the telephone line. The system requires that the television set and the telephone lines be near or next to each other. There are, in other words, significant operational problems inherent in the use of videotex services. Thus we assign usage difficulty a high score of 9.

Value

Perhaps the second biggest hurdle to the adoption of videotex is that it offers neither performance nor price value to the consumer. Existing alternatives are quite satisfactory for banking, shopping, information acquisition, and education. As with automatic teller machines, discussed earlier, it probably offers a time value, since videotex services can be used virtually at any time of the day or night. This convenience is, however, offset by the extra price as well as the extra effort required for transactions. Value barriers rise to a high score of 9.

Risk

There is significant perceived risk associated with videotex. People worry about rapid obsolescence of the existing technology as well as performance uncertainty. Will the bank transaction really be carried by videotex? Will I be overcharged? Maybe I will abuse the system or maybe the children will play with it. Will the right merchandise come if I order it by videotex? These, and many more concerns, are often revealed in focus group interviews. High risk measures out to a score of 8.

Tradition

Because Americans love gadgets, new technologies, and modern ways of doing things, one would expect no tradition barrier for videotex, but this is not universally true. Although yuppies may love the modern technology, a vast percentage of the mass market is culturally resistant to computers and high technology. In fact, members of the great American public have a fear of modern or futuristic technology. Our score on tradition barrier, therefore, is a medium 5.

Image

Fortunately, videotex seems to carry no negative stereotypes. It is, however, apparently considered a highly discretionary and conspicuous-consumption service to be indulged in by the wealthy, an association that could limit its mass market appeal. We give image an invitingly low score of 2.

The total customer barrier score is, however, a discouraging 33 out of 50. Together, customer and corporate barriers rate a daunting 65 out of a possible 100.

ISDN

The letters ISDN stand for integrated services defined network. Although initially intended for business customers, ISDN is a universal service from the sender to the receiver of information and integrates all types of information communication. In other words, it extends the telephone capabilities of switching, transport, and signaling from voice to data, pictures, and text with equal ease as well as simultaneously mixing and matching different types of information over the same telecommunications network.

This network thus represents a major technological evolution in telecommunications. It requires the development of a totally new central office switch, a new PBX, and new desktop telephone sets that probably will not look like the traditional telephone sets. In addition, the new network may require higher capacity transport channels, such as fiber optics, although it is capable of using the existing twisted pair of copper wires.

Let us examine the corporate and customer barriers associated with ISDN.

Expertise

Most manufacturers are finding out that ISDN is an extremely difficult technology. Even though global standards have been established by CCITT, the complexity of the layers of information and intelligence to be stored, switched, and transported is enormous. Even though more than a decade of R&D work has gone into its development, ISDN is still at an experimental stage. The new network also requires a high degree of integration between computer and communications technologies. Unfortunately, the history of coexistence between these two disciplines is not encouraging. Integration will be extremely difficult. Score 9 for a high expertise barrier.

Operations

The ISDN operations, especially at the telephone company level, are not compatible with older technologies. Replacing the central office switchboard and rewiring the corporate office are required to utilize ISDN capabilities. Furthermore, to fully exploit ISDN's potential, it is often desirable, if not always necessary, to replace copper wire with fiber optics. Our score for the operations barrier is therefore 8.

Resources

Even though other barriers are high, financial resources are likely to generate the greatest corporate resistance. At the manufacturing level, several giant corporations, including ITT and Siemens, have been forced to establish strategic alliances to share the resource burden. At the telephone company level, companies will have to invest a massive amount of new capital to install this technology. And nobody has as yet even attempted to come out with desktop terminals suitable for ISDN architecture. Those costs are yet to be determined. The resource barrier rates a perfect—or, rather, imperfect—10.

Regulation

There is a significant international issue involved in what is, after all, an international network. Ironically, it is manifested at the local telephone company level. The Europeans would prefer the local telephone companies to also supply customer-premises equipment such as PBXs, telephone sets, and key systems along with the network services. On the other hand, in the United States and several other countries, supplying the equipment in the customer's office, including the PBX, is a deregulated and highly competitive business. This conflict has created regulatory uncertainty as to where the interface between network and terminal equipment should be housed. Should the hookup be at the telephone company, and thus a regulated service; or should it be at the customer's place of business, in equipment available from a number of unregulated vendors? The uncertainty translates into a regulatory barrier of 5.

Market Access

Market access is a hard barrier to evaluate. On the one hand, access is protected by the local telephone companies, who act as the safekeepers and are difficult to bypass, especially in the ISDN environment. On the other hand, the local telephone companies have expressed serious interest in introducing the ISDN technology themselves to the corporate end users, thus becoming competitors. In fact, most of them are already having trials in key cities and with key customers. Unfortunately, ISDN is not a universally accepted technology. Furthermore, the local telephone companies worry about the capital they have already sunk into this venture. Balancing all the factors, we score a 5 for market access.

Corporate barriers rise to a high total of 37 out of 50. Let us now examine the customer resistance to ISDN. We define end-user corporations as the customers of this innovation.

Usage

The ISDN system requires an almost total change in the customer's organization. Corporations must buy new terminal equipment, perhaps rewire the buildings, definitely train the employees, and most likely reorganize the physical facilities around the new technology. In short, ISDN mandates a massive change from current operations because it is not fully compatible with existing office or factory communication technologies at the user level. Thus, the usage barrier rates a 9.

Value

One of the biggest barriers for ISDN is its value to the users. Although the new network has significantly greater capabilities than existing technologies, many experts are not sure that the extra capital costs involved justify the value-added functions and features. Furthermore, some experts even believe that the extra communication capabilities of ISDN will probably never be used by the customers, since a better educated work force is needed to fully engage the technology. In short, ISDN suffers from the same problems as office automation or factory automation. The value barrier is a moderately high 7.

Risk

The primary risk associated with the adoption of ISDN technology is the potential disruption of business operations and subsequent loss of work days. If the transition is not smooth, significant foulups are likely to occur in all phases of the business. Furthermore, because ISDN is an integrated technology, the corporation perceives that it is putting all its eggs in one basket. The essential response to ISDN implementation will be and must be crisis management. In short, the risk of failure is high. Our score on this barrier is, therefore, 8.

Tradition

The ISDN system also imposes a new corporate culture. All involved personnel must be trained to use a single terminal for voice, data, and video information. Work flows, employee relationships, and work practices will be affected. Management must, for instance, integrate the telecommunications department and the computer department (data processing people). They are at present separate and report to two different organizations. This changes the relationship between departments and employees; who reports to whom becomes an issue. The tradition-based resistance will be high; the barrier is thus rated 8.

Image

While ISDN does not have an image problem as such, there is always resistance to a new technology. Those senior executives who do not believe in "new-fangled" ways of doing business will probably have negative feelings for ISDN similar to their attitudes about computers and factory automation. The image barrier is not, however, overwhelming. Our score is, therefore, 3.

The total ISDN score for customer resistance is 35 out of 50. The combined score for both corporate and customer resistance is 72 out of 100, which is even higher than the impediment to videotex.

ELECTRONIC MAIL

Electronic mail refers to nonvoice, two-way, end-to-end communication between any two parties with the use of a cathode-ray tube (CRT) terminal and a modem (the central component of a computer and a connection device to a phone). It is equivalent to mail because the sender and the receiver do not need to be physically present or electronically connected at the same time to communicate with each other. Of course, electronic mail can also be used strictly as a one-way communication from a single sender to all the receivers—as with internal company memos, newsletters, and general announcements—using messages transmitted by and stored in a computer instead of papers physically delivered and piled on a desk.

Electronic Mail

Our analysis suggests that there are lower corporate barriers to product development but greater barriers to market development. It is relatively easy for firms to offer electronic mail, but quite difficult for the customers to embrace it. Let us discuss the disparity in some detail, beginning with the structural corporate barriers.

Expertise

The technical expertise required to offer electronic mail service is already in place. It is fairly reliable, has relatively few compatibility problems, and very few interfacing problems from one component to another. It is easy to integrate into the known and embedded technologies of computers and telecommunications. The U.S. postal service even created a hybrid service called E-Com that integrated electronic mail with regular postal delivery to reach the mass market for distribution of junk mail. The only unique aspect of electronic mail that requires some learning concerns electronic storage and forwarding. This easy hurdle gives a score of 2 to the expertise barrier.

Operations

Providing electronic mail service as a part of telecommunications services is not very difficult either for the corporation's network operations people or for their sales and service people. It integrates with existing business operations easily. The only unique problems may be related to the software and to the database management techniques, both of which are within the capabilities of the providers. Again, the score is 2.

Resources

The capital resources needed to offer electronic mail are substantial. However, they are minimal compared to the even bigger capital expenditures the industry must invest in central office switches and local loops. Therefore, electronic mail does not create a massive resource deployment problem for most large telephone or computer companies. While it is not a *relatively* high investment, electronic mail does represent a large commitment in *absolute* dollars, as companies like Satellite Business Systems have discovered. The large satellite communication firm, now owned by MCI, has drained more than one wealthy parent. The capital resources barrier must be rated a moderate 5.

Regulation

Regulation is only a problem for the Bell Operating Companies, which are not allowed to be in enhanced telecommunications services. Our score for the regulation barrier is 2.

Market Access

The market access barrier is also low. Most corporate customers can be reached by all the major providers of electronic mail. Most of these firms—including all major office equipment vendors, computer vendors, and telecommunications vendors—have their own sales and service organizations close to the customer. Our score on market access is only 1.

The total resistance for electronic mail with respect to corporate barriers is an inviting 12 out of 50. The customer barriers constitute the real impediment to the innovation.

Usage

The biggest customer barrier has to do with usage patterns. Most office workers are not trained to use electronic mail. Beside training employees, corporations must install the required spe-

Electronic Mail

cial equipment. Implementation takes discipline and conscious effort because the existing alternatives (face to face or telephone communications) are quite viable, easier to use, and very familiar. We rate the usage barrier a 7.

Value

The value of electronic mail to the corporation and its employees is problematic. On the one hand, it does increase the communication efficiency, especially on the time and distance dimensions. On the other hand, electronic mail forces some trade-offs. For example, it is more formal, more standardized, and definitely less personal. Because electronic mail consists of written messages that are stored and retrieved, there is some potential threat to confidentiality. Although, electronic mail has the performance value, it does not necessarily have the price value. The customer has to invest significant amounts of capital in the terminals to make the system function throughout the corporation. By the same token, if a company already has enough terminals, including personal computers, the add-on cost of electronic mail is insignificant and therefore possesses high price value. All things considered, the value barrier is a 6.

Risk

Most people experience some degree of risk when using electronic mail. The new technology evokes fears of being considered incompetent, of sending the wrong messages to the wrong parties, of having messages not reach the intended party for whatever reason, and of failing to cope in general. Although the perception of risk vanishes with experience, it is a major hurdle to sign up a potential customer. The difficulty is further compounded by the relatively risk-free character of existing alternatives. Our score for the perceived risk barrier is an 8.

Tradition

The same problem exists with respect to corporate culture and traditions. Most office workers love to interact with each other in person. Personal communication enables them to express themselves with gestures and other forms of body language. It allows them to gather or disseminate information in a more customized or selective way. Personal communications permit people to express emotions, feelings, and many other qualities, which is simply not possible in electronic mail. Finally, corporate culture often makes it difficult, if not impossible, to communicate in writing. Most confidential communications (even rumors) are spoken, not written. The tradition barrier is formidable; we give it an 8.

Image

Electronic mail does not seem to suffer from any significant image problem. In some sense, it might even have a positive image, as something a more modern adaptive manager who is with the times would use. As we said earlier, perhaps the only resistance might come from more traditional managers, who have a negative image about all modern technologies. This barrier rates only a 2.

The total score on customer barriers is 31 out of 50, a significant percentage of the combined score of 43. Customer resistance, rather than corporate structure, is the threat to this innovation.

LIFELINE SERVICE

Lifeline service refers to a basic level of telephone service. It consists of providing universal access for both incoming and outgoing calls—the customer can call anywhere; anyone can

Lifeline Service

call in—but the customer must pay for each local call beyond a certain minimum number, which includes emergency calls for police, fire, and ambulance. It is designed primarily for the poor, who can no longer afford the rising costs of plain old telephone service thanks to the regulatory processes, which have eliminated, at least partially, the cross subsidies from long distance calls and from business customers.

Lifeline service is sometimes referred to as local measured service (LMS), although the two may not be comparable in their prices from state to state. In California and other states, Lifeline service is mandated by law to ensure that no one is denied basic telephone service because of affordability problems. It is a subsidized service because it is priced below cost, and it is identical in quality to the regular, fixed-rate, unlimited-calling service to which most people subscribe.

Our examination of the corporate and customer barriers to this new class of service indicates, once again, very low corporate resistance but high resistance from customers. Let's look at the corporate structural barriers first.

Expertise

Lifeline service requires no new expertise for the phone company. In fact, it is primarily a pricing mechanism and, at most, requires proper billing, collection, and account management. Since most of this is well within the capabilities of local telephone companies, our difficulty rating for overcoming the expertise barrier is 1.

Operations

Minimal software and account management changes are necessary to offer this service. The technical quality is comparable to all other residential local services. It does require keeping track of customers who are eligible to receive the subsidy, but the record-keeping would not be so different from that needed for other groups of customers with which the telephone company does business. Since Lifeline service is easy to incorporate into the existing operations, our score for the operations barrier is also 1.

Resources

There are no resource implications since this is not a new offering as such but simply a repricing of an existing service. The local phone company must, however, assess the impact of Lifeline on existing revenues because customers who are currently paying higher prices for the flat-rate, unlimited-calling service can now choose the lower priced basic service at substantial savings. However, the group of customers who would be eligible represents less than 10 percent of the total of all residential customer, assuming membership is to be determined by the federal government's poverty guidelines. Most of the phone company's revenues come from business and residential customers above the poverty line who purchase a variety of specialized calling services. Therefore, the impact of Lifeline on revenues is less than critical to corporate survival. Score 1 for the resource barrier.

Regulation

State regulation has actually encouraged the local telephone companies to offer Lifeline services. In some states, Lifeline has even been mandated. At the same time, the regulatory process for setting the rates and for establishing the eligibility criteria is frustrating and involves additional effort. Even then, local telephone companies are very experienced with the regulatory process of rate setting, although there may be more emotions involved in the issue of subsidizing the poor. Overall, we believe it is not a major barrier and, therefore, our score is again 1.

Market Access

Finally, we do not believe local telephone companies need contend with any significant market access barrier. They can easily assign the Lifeline service to needy customers by making a change in their service records. Alternatively, they can inform the target group that they have a choice between Lifeline and the regular-priced, flat-rate service. No matter how you measure it, market access is not a barrier and, therefore, our score is 1.

Corporate barriers total only 5 out of a possible 50. The five customer barriers, however, constitute a greater hindrance.

Usage

The residential customer who has been accustomed to making unlimited calls of varying lengths is now restricted to far fewer calls of probably very short duration, since each additional call and each additional minute will cost extra money. Lifeline will make a significant change in their calling patterns and habits. In fact, it is possible that some customers may actually end up paying a higher total bill for Lifeline if their unlimited usage has been excessive and they do *not* change. The poor, or many of them, must adapt to save money on the service. The potential conflict with preferred life-style and behavior will erect a usage barrier high enough to score a 6.

Value

Ironically, the Lifeline service may not be valuable to the target population, even though it is low priced. First, most poor people tend to live in small geographically concentrated areas. Therefore, their community of interest is highly local rather than national. Second, they tend to have strong interpersonal relationships or social interactions with friends, family members, and caretakers. This, too, generates a need for extra local calling. Finally, they are likely to have a greater amount of discretionary time on their hands due to their work style and life-style. In other words, what they need is a telephone service that has an *unlimited* number of permissible calls rather than restricted calling patterns! Unless both the regulation and the local telephone companies agree to offer them the regular, flat-rate, unlimited calling service at significant subsidies, it will not be in the interest of the poor to subscribe to LMS, or Lifeline service.

No wonder, therefore, that when some local telephone companies offered a highly affordable LMS, there were very few subscribers from the target population. Instead, dual-income, career-oriented, white-collar young households with no children were found to be the major subscribers to LMS! And that makes sense. This group has a community of interest that is more national in scope than local. Our score on the value barrier, therefore, is another 8.

Risk

The primary risk faced by prospective users is that they will have to identify themselves as poor to the regulatory agency in charge of determining eligibility. (The local phone companies will stay away from that decision.) The certification process may result in the government's involvement in personal and financial matters. This makes some people uncomfortable. We are quite sure that many poor people who are immigrants to this country will have strong anxieties about going through the eligibility process. Our score on risk is, therefore, also 6.

Tradition

We also think that residential customers who opt for the Lifeline service will face the same psychological and cultural dilemma people have had to meet when accepting other socially subsi-

Digital Centrex

dized services such as welfare, food stamps, and public housing. Most of them feel a sense of guilt and shame: for example, an estimated half of the eligible people do not take advantage of the food stamps program even after they have been made aware of its availability. Psychological and social discomfort creates a resistance we measure at 6.

Image

As mentioned above, declaring oneself poor has considerable negative connotations in our society. It suggests a defeatist attitude and a lack of motivation; it creates suspicions of fraud. The negative images associated with public assistance programs—and the LMS is one such program—are strong and debilitating. We therefore rate the image barrier 8.

The scores on the customer barriers add up to a total of 34 out of 50. Adding in the corporate total of 5 yields 39 of a possible 100. Thus, the Lifeline service encounters low corporate barriers but is thwarted by high customer resistance.

DIGITAL CENTREX

Digital centrex is the name of an upgraded technology designed to compete against the new-generation PBX switches that are installed in corporations to handle a variety of telecommunication operations. A centrex or PBX provides services such as intercom, receptionist functions, party-on-hold, call transfers, and three-way conference calls that make both intracompany communication and outside communication more flexible and more convenient. Centrex and PBX represent a very popular service package, especially to large organizations that have thousands of telephone lines.

A centrex system requires no equipment at the customer's office; regular telephone sets are adequate. All the electronic intelligence needed to perform the desired functions is located in the central office of the telephone company. A PBX does the same thing, but it is expensive equipment bought by the customer that requires installation and maintenance. Thus, the corporation can either pay lots of money up front in buying PBX and save on the telephone line charges (this is because the PBX can concentrate the number of lines to be used by several people), or it can use centrex and continue to pay each user's telephone line charge to the phone company but avoid the capital cost of PBX as well as its maintenance. The PBX is like a very large computer and must be maintained.

The old centrex service came up against strong competition from a new generation of digital PBX systems that could perform not only all centrex functions, but others, such as security and energy management (especially suitable for hotels and motels). Furthermore, the new PBX was a lot cheaper to operate because it reduced the number of lines for outside communication. In many ways, the central office technology seemed to have fallen behind the customer-premises technology for the first time.

In response to this challenge, local telephone companies have attempted to upgrade their central office technology so that they can offer digital centrex services with a host of additional features not available in the older technology. In general, digital centrex is at least comparable to digital PBX; in fact, it might possibly offer additional flexibility and features above and beyond digital PBX. As we shall see, however, this new technology must contend with high corporate barriers.

Expertise

The expertise required to install and operate a new class of central office technology is quite complex and different from that needed for the old system, especially in relation to the

Digital Centrex

software and database management functions. At the same time, it is attainable. Furthermore, the switch manufacturers (AT&T and Northern Telecom) have most of the know-how, although the local telephone companies will have to acquire it as they buy and install the new switches. Our score of 5 on the expertise barrier reflects this middling-to-tough obstacle.

Operations

Installing the new switch with digital centrex capabilities represents a major deviation from existing operations. It means removing the existing equipment and associated technical support and documentation and replacing it with a more complex switch. There are significant operations barriers in the process, including disrupting normal telephone service, coordinating with the phone company, assigning new numbers to each user, creating a billing system, and so on. Although the same physical facilities can be used to change over to the new switch, it is still a massive disruption. Our score on the operations barrier is, therefore, 7.

Resources

Digital centrex requires massive resource commitment up front. The commitment is also long term because the depreciation schedules for central office equipment are spread out over an extended period. Many local telephone companies simply do not have the capital resources to fund the new generation central office switches to offer digital centrex services. These restraints produce a score of 8 for the resource barrier.

Regulation

Although there are no regulatory restrictions to impede digital centrex services, implementation of the innovation will mean a considerable amount of regulatory work. Digital is a migration technology; it offers more values and features that make the older analog central services obsolete. It is not clear whether local regulators are sympathetic to the phone companies' plan to write off the embedded costs of the older switches in favor of the new switches. And even if the regulators agree, it is not clear whether there is even enough demand to justify offering digital centrex services. The muddle produces a score of 5 for the regulatory barrier.

Market Access

There are some serious market access barriers to digital centrex. First of all, corporate customers that have a PBX switch on their facilities are unlikely to transfer to digital centrex because they must give up capitalized assets at or below book value. Furthermore, they may not be able to switch to the local telephone exchange's centrex service without facing the nightmare of reconfiguring telephone lines and numbers. Second, the declining cost of the terminals may make buying the terminals and writing off the purchase using accelerated depreciation more economical than renting them from the local telephone company as part of the digital centrex package. Finally, there is strong competition from PBX manufacturers also trying to upgrade customers to the fourth-generation PBX, which has added capabilities for data communication, such as local area networking (LAN), and can operate as a hub for building private networks.

Of course, there is no market access problem in terms of channels of distribution. Local telephone companies have direct access to corporate customers and in that sense can always offer the digital centrex services. At the same time, digital centrex capabilities probably require greater coordination between the telecommunications manager and the data processing manager,

Digital Centrex

which was not essential when the older analog centrex services were offered. Overall, our score on market access is 7.

The total for all five corporate barriers is 32 out of a possible 50, indicating substantial structural resistance. Analysis of the customer barriers paints a brighter picture.

Usage

Part of the good news is that customers need not make significant changes in their usage patterns. If anything, the new digital centrex services are more convenient and more flexible. They also offer more of the features and functions people like and need in telecommunications networks. Indeed, the current customers for analog centrex can easily transfer their usage procedures to the digital centrex services. The usage barrier, therefore, rates at only a 2.

Value

Perhaps the biggest customer barrier may relate to the issue of value. One has to consider several questions. Does the customer really need the additional capabilities provided by digital PBX? Are they paying a higher price by being on the leading edge of technology relative to future customers? Is digital centrex a greater performance value than the existing centrex or, alternatively, the digital PBX? Unless digital centrex is priced low enough to create a comparative value for the customer, it will encounter customer resistance of at least moderate intensity. That makes this barrier score a 5.

Risk

Because they are dealing with leading-edge technology, customers may worry whether local telephone companies have really mastered the innovation or whether they, the customers, will become the guinea pigs in the company's trial-and-error learning. They are also concerned that the new-generation technology will significantly change and, therefore, require upgrading in a very short period of time. Fortunately, digital centrex is a service and, therefore, requires much less capital commitment by the customer. The local telephone company must assume the financial risk, although we expect a multiyear contractual agreement to be part of the initial offering. Overall, we believe the risks are, at worst, moderate and, therefore, our score for this barrier is 4.

Tradition

There are no real tradition barriers. As mentioned earlier, digital centrex may require some degree of coordination between the departments, but it does not mandate massive reorganization, at least for existing centrex users. In other words, migration to the newer technology is not likely to be disrupted by corporate culture resistance. Once again, we meet an easy hurdle to leap; our score is 2.

Image

Digital centrex has no image problems. If anything, *digital* means more modern, better capability, and more features. Therefore, the new service might even have some positive associations. We give the image barrier an inviting score of 1, which is more a bump than a barrier.

Overall, the customer barrier adds up to only 14 out of 50. The real impediment seems to be the high corporate barriers (32 out of 50). Total ranking of the difficulty facing the innovation is 46 out of 100.

CELLULAR MOBILE TELEPHONES

Cellular mobile phone service is a major technological innovation that allows owners, in theory, to keep in touch with the world from any place outside the home or office. So far, however, the phones must be in a car to function, although very soon people might be able to carry a cellular mobile telephone in their pockets and briefcases.

Unlike regular telephones, which require hard wires to connect with the telephone exchange, the cellular mobile phone uses the airwaves to send or receive calls. It needs special and dedicated electronic switches and low-power antennae to link up with the network. This equipment must be set up every 5 to 10 miles. Each switch with its antenna is a cell that can connect with a fixed capacity of calls at any one time. If a given cell's capacity is saturated, however, it is relatively easy to expand the capacity of incoming and outgoing calls by splitting the cell. In theory, the capacity of the cellular mobile phone for a given geographical area is unlimited, which makes it far more flexible than the standard wired-phone technology. Furthermore, since the technology is based on electronics, its costs should enjoy very sharp experience curves, ultimately resulting in a rapid reduction in manufacturing costs for the switch as well as for the phone instruments. In fact, most experts believe that the cellular mobile phone will have the same dramatic price reduction and feature enhancements as electronic calculators and digital watches.

Cellular mobile telephone service is under the jurisdiction of the Federal Communications Commission (FCC) in the United States. The FCC has licensed two operators in each of 120 U.S. cities. Usually, one operator is the traditional local telephone company (wireline company) and the other is a nontelephone company approved by the FCC and selected from several applicants by a lottery system.

As with the digital centrex, cellular mobile phone service faces high resistance from corporate structural barriers and low resistance from its potential customers. As usual, we will begin with the corporate analysis.

Expertise

Cellular mobile phone service institutes a total departure from the traditional offerings. New expertise is needed both to build the equipment and to operate the system. Hardware manufacturers such as AT&T, Motorola, and Oki have had to develop fresh R&D approaches, different manufacturing capacities, and new software systems. Similarly, service providers, including local telephone companies, have had to learn new customer service skills. They have had to master a new billing process, selling through resellers, and pricing different options to meet or create demand. Consequently, our score for the expertise barrier is 7, indicating moderately tough resistance.

Operations

The cellular mobile service does not blend easily into the existing system of operations. It is a separate, stand-alone business with its own dedicated hardware, software, and customer service operations. The problem can be traced in part to the regulatory mandate to form a separate subsidiary. There is also a lack of continuity between existing wireline operations and the cellular operations. Of course, the cellular mobile network interfaces with the regular copper wire network to provide universal access to all telephone users. But it doesn't come easily. Our score for the operations barrier is 9.

Resources

Cellular mobile telephone service is the product of a technology alternative to copper wire, but it essentially performs the

Cellular Mobile Telephones

same functions. Therefore, it requires massive capitalization. As a result, many companies that won the lottery for the right to operate the service have formed joint ventures with other organizations to increase their financial stability. Furthermore, within a very short history of five years, the industry has undergone national or regional consolidation, especially among the nonwire companies. In short, building and operating a cellular mobile telephone service digs deeply into corporate pockets. The resource barrier is high: 8.

Regulation

As we have mentioned, the FCC regulates the business. Currently, only two companies are allowed to operate in any one geographical area. However, as the cellular mobile network becomes national in scope, similar to the paging business, the regulatory picture could change. It is quite possible that cellular mobile phones may become a long distance network and compete freely with the existing long distance carriers. The regulatory barriers are also low because the FCC permits pricing competition between two carriers and, of course, because the telephone-set market is fully deregulated. This barrier rates only a 3.

Market Access

In contrast, market access is a significant barrier to the innovation. For example, existing automobiles are not designed to accommodate the cellular telephone. Furthermore, unlike the car radio or tape deck, which are universally accepted as standard options, the car telephone is considered by some to be a road hazard, since it requires significant concentration and may distract the driver. Automobile companies have not as yet made it a readily available accessory, although some analysts forecast such a development before 1990. In addition, distribution channels are already in place and there is strong competition between vendors. However, the mobile phone must be custom installed, and to that extent, it is not as easy to acquire as regular telephone service. Balancing all these factors, we score market access a moderate 5.

Corporate barriers total out to a formidable 32 out of 50. Happily, the customer barriers are less imposing.

Usage

The cellular telephone works the same way as the regular telephone. It requires no user training, and all the skills of regular telephone operation are transferable. People feel comfortable right from the beginning with the familiar voice technology. The customized installation in the vehicle represents the only inconvenience. Numerous suppliers mitigate the strain, however. The usage barrier offers a meager resistance of 2.

Value

Unlike many other consumer telecommunications innovations, including the legendary picture phone, the cellular mobile telephone appears to have good relative value. It is a great time utilization device because it allows time-driven people to put what is often idle time in their car to productive use. This quality is especially appealing to certain time-sensitive professionals like doctors, executives, salespeople, and contractors. Second, the mobile phone is a very valuable product/service in emergencies. Doctors use it to remain constantly within reach of hospitals and clinics, just as they use their paging device. Of course, any motorist might find it a very useful device after a breakdown or accident—so much so that, as noted earlier, the cellular mobile telephone should become a common car accessory. While the costs of equipment and the service fees are now significantly higher than regular telephones or even public telephones, those costs will decline, and the mobile phone will become a univer-

Cellular Mobile Telephones

sal service. The value barrier is, therefore, now a 3—and steadily dropping.

Risk

The consumer does face some economic risk. One may waste the money spent on the equipment because of possible early obsolesence. Also, new features and better prices are likely to prevail in the future. Indeed, the industry expects the instrument set to be available for as little as $250 by 1988! The financial risk associated with the cellular mobile telephone has encouraged many consumers to postpone their purchase, just as they did with the VCR and the personal computer. However, service providers are offering the sets on a lease basis in order to minimize the financial risk. The barrier is crumbling; it is now down to 2.

Tradition

Traditions should not offer much resistance, either. One can stretch the point and argue that the normal behavior of listening to the radio while driving has to give way in order to use the telephone, but it is a minor adjustment. The familiar telephone set, the good quality of the reception, and full network access make the cellular mobile system a perfect substitute for the regular telephone. Our score on tradition is 1.

Image

Cellular mobile phones do not suffer from any bad associations. It is, in fact, a conspicuous-consumption product and service. Many early customers have been known to make calls to their friends and coworkers just to let everyone know that *they* are on top of the cellular mobile technology. What image barrier? Give it a score of 1.

The total impediment created by customer barriers is a very low 9 out of 50—contrasting with a total corporate resistance of 32. The combined score of 41 suggests a moderately difficult road for this innovation. A much easier path can be predicted for two other telecommunications services that face low corporate and customer barriers.

TOLL-FREE SERVICES

The toll-free call, with the 800 area code, is by now a common phenomenon. It was designed originally to mechanize long distance collect calls that had to be handled by an operator. The innovation became necessary when hotels and airlines began to advertise that customers could call collect to make reservations. Unfortunately, the costs of operator-handled calls were increasing for the telephone company without proportionate increases in rates. The combination of greater volume and declining revenue forced a search for savings through automation. The Bell System was already offering the WATS service, which allowed customers to call out without regard to distance and time because they were being charged by volume of usage. It was relatively easy therefore for the Bell System to offer inward WATS, in which charges were made to the business called (hotel or airline, for instance) instead of to the people originating the call. This inverted WATS line service eventually evolved into the 800-number system, with newer applications and features. And, as we shall see, this service had *very low* corporate and customer barriers to overcome.

Expertise

Bell had to devise a unique system for call billing and detailing (tracking call times and length, and the number of calls from designated areas) to fit the 800-number service. Fortunately, they had related experience and expertise gained through years of operator-handled calls, as well as through their regular WATS service. In other words, the 800-number service was more of a continuous evolution than a discontinuous revolution in technology. Our rating for the expertise barrier is, therefore, 2.

Operations

The changes required in company operations to offer the 800-number services were also minimal. It was simply one additional innovative service that could be performed with ease by the existing network. The operations barrier score is the lowest possible: 1.

Resources

The 800-number service required only a moderate amount of resources to create the unique software, billing, and data management systems, and since the service involved only one more use of the central office switch, no large up-front capital outlay was needed. Therefore, our score on the resource barrier is only 2.

Regulation

Both local and national regulators were interested in mechanizing collect calls because the change benefited the public. It shifted the costs of those calls from the consumer to the business corporation, which could write them off as tax deductible expenses. Indeed, the 800-number service clearly established a win-win-win situation the people who used the service (they called free), the telephone company (it made money), and the corporate customers for the service (their businesses were stimulated). As a result, no real regulatory barriers were erected to block the innovative service—a fact reflected in our score of 2.

Market Access

The Bell System suffered no market access problems. The same direct sales force that offered WATS lines, private lines, and other interacting services could easily sell the 800-number service. It required no new channels to reach the customer. Furthermore, Bell needed to make only slight changes in customer organization. The market access barrier goes no higher than 1.

The total score for the corporate barriers adds up to only 8 out of 50. The customer barriers also offer little resistance.

Usage

The 800-number service has several advantages over operator-handled collect calls: it is automatic, it allows callers to wait if company operators are busy, and it provides detailed information on call volume. The service is also more convenient and more flexible. People have, for instance, an easier time remembering a standard 800 area code. As businesses became more sophisticated in using the service, they began asking for phone numbers to follow 800 that could be represented by letter combinations related to the company: 800-HOLIDAY for reservations at Holiday Inns, for example.

The only usage problem associated with the 800-number service was at the receiving end, when too many calls were made at one time, causing delays. Bell has had to adapt distribution technology to sequence the calls. Our score for the usage barrier is 2.

Value

This is one telecommunications innovation that seems to have considerable value to both public users and corporate customers. It creates, as we mentioned earlier, a winning situation for all parties. Without exaggeration, we can think of the 800-number service as the nylon or the baking soda of the

Toll-Free Services 131

telecommunications business: Customers are likely to discover applications and uses of the service in situations never imagined by the originating firm. Witness the use of the 800 number for customer complaints, shareholder relations, disaster assistance, political campaigns, as well as fundraising for charities! In our analysis, the 800-number service has great performance and price value that should sustain it over a comparatively long life cycle. We rate value resistance at 2.

Risk

The risk to the corporate customer is also minimal. As with WATS lines, the convenience of the toll-free number increases the volume of calling and, therefore, the cost to the business with the 800 number is greater—but then, so are the sales generated by the service. Having an 800 number also means capital investment (an economic risk) for the automatic call distributor equipment, especially for high-volume calling, as in the airlines business. Since the customer does not have to worry that the system might not work or that the technology might become obsolete, the risk barrier is quite small: 2.

Tradition

Since the service upgraded familiar collect-call procedures already in place, it did not require any corporate culture changes regarding customer handling. In fact, the 800 system simply eliminated the interruption by the telephone operator asking for consent to complete the calls. Score 1 for minimum disruption.

Image

The 800-number service actually enhances the image of the company that has it. The service suggests that because the corporation is willing to encourage calling, it is customer-oriented and willing to provide service. Positive associations make our score 1 for this nonbarrier.

The total score for all five customer barriers is the same 8 out of 50 racked up by the corporate barriers. A grand total of 16 (of 100) indicates an innovation with little in its path to success.

CUSTOM CALLING SERVICES

Custom calling services (CCS) refer to a collection of features added on to basic telephone service. They include such attractive services as call waiting, call forwarding, and three-way calling. Call waiting signals that another caller is trying to reach you while you are already on the line talking to someone else. It allows you to put the first caller on hold, answer the incoming second call, and come back to the first party. It thus eliminates the busy signal and makes sure you don't miss any important calls. If you have call forwarding, you can program your telephone so that incoming calls can be transferred to another number at a distant location where you can be reached. Three-way calling, as the name implies, allows simultaneous conversation between three parties anywhere in the country. Many additional value-added services are currently being planned as part of a CCS package. As with the 800 service for businesses, CCS faces little hindrance from either corporate or customer structural barriers.

Expertise

Most of the technical expertise needed for CCS is already available in the new electronic switches. Therefore, the local telephone company must only develop the software, customer service procedures, and database management system to offer CCS.

Custom Calling Services

Since most of this know-how is already available to the engineers within the network planning group, the expertise barrier rates but a 1 for difficulty.

Operations

Custom calling services requires no major changes in telephone company operations. Of course, the company needs to tariff the service (that is, apply to the local regulators for permission to offer the service at a specified price), offer it to the customers, and ensure that proper billing and collection takes place. However, all of these additional activities can easily be accommodated within the existing operations. Since there is little operational drag, our score here is 1.

Resources

The additional resources required to offer these discretionary value-added services are minimal. As mentioned earlier, they require, at most, new software and database management capabilities, which are available within the existing resource base of the local telephone company. Once again, little structural resistance equates to a low difficulty score of 1.

Regulation

Since CCS is a part of the local exchange service, it is under the jurisdiction of the public utility commission of each state. Most states have allowed CCS on a tariffed basis, and the higher profit margins generated by CCS are expected to subsidize the basic telephone service. Therefore, local regulators have been favorable toward the innovative package. For regulatory barriers, the score is 1.

Market Access

There are no significant market access barriers. All customers currently served by the new electronic switching systems (ESS) can easily subscribe to the CCS package. Unfortunately, CCS cannot be made available to those customers who are now served by the old electromechanical cross-bar or step-function switches. In general, market access is not a problem for CCS. The score is 2.

The total score for all five corporate barriers is an almost trivial 6 out of 50. The customer barriers are almost as negligible.

Usage

There are, for instance, virtually no barriers created by established usage patterns. Most custom calling services use the existing telephone instruments and require no modifications. All the changes are software driven and can be performed in the telephone company's database systems. The customer can stand pat. More good news is that CCS features are simple to use. They require no extensive education or training. Customers need only read instructions and press touchtone buttons. Obviously, they will have to own touchtone phones and, as mentioned above, they must be in a community served by an ESS switch. Usage barriers should not present a problem. Our score is 1.

Value

Not all custom calling services possess significant value relative to basic phone service because of the extra monthly fees. Most individual services are priced between $1.50 and $3.00 per month. As a result, a large majority of residential customers do not subscribe to call forwarding, probably because they see no value in transferring calls to another number in case they are away. On the other hand, call waiting is highly popular, especially among households with teenage children. Indeed, it often becomes a necessity, because teenagers are constantly on the phone in the evening. Its value is very high to any adult who wants to maintain access to the outside world while at home. By and large, however, customers have been slow to accept several service options. The value barrier does, therefore, offer moderate resistance to the innovation; we give it a 4.

Risk

There are virtually no risks involved with CCS. Each of the individual services is available on a monthly fee basis, and the cost of canceling any of them is not high. Nor are there performance risks, because people trust telephone technology. Once again, the barrier score is 1.

Tradition

The service should not disrupt anyone's life-style. In fact, it may enhance the quality of life by increasing the chance that people will be able to talk with each other without delays. Some business customers, however, have terminated the call waiting service because they find call interruption annoying. The call waiting feature could also disconnect a linked-up computer. This problem has been solved recently with adjustments to the modem. We think the tradition barrier rates only a 1.

Image

If anything, custom calling services reflect a modern, positive image. There are no negative stereotypes, except perhaps those associated with gadgets and highly discretionary consumption. Overall, we believe the image barriers are minimal, and our score is 1.

The total score for the customer barriers to CCS totals only 8 out of 50. When added to the corporate score of 6, the grand measure of structural resistance facing CCS is a far from daunting 14.

SUMMARY

We have attempted to demonstrate that the quality of corporate and customer barriers tends to vary across innovations within the same industry. We selected the telecommunications industry because it is universal and because it is generating a large number of product and service innovations: videotex, ISDN, electronic mail, Lifeline service, digital centrex, cellular mobile phones, 800-number service, and custom calling services. Half of these are for business customers; the other half are designed for residential users.

We also attempted to measure the difficulty of introducing the innovations into the marketplace by rating the strength of each of the 10 structural barriers for each of the new products or services.* Our analysis was designed to give both a general assessment of each innovation's potentials and a breakdown by barrier of the chief impediments. Table 4.1 summarizes the results.

Part 2 of the book demonstrates the use of this exercise. Depending on the nature of the resistance, one can select a strategy appropriate for launching an innovative product or service. The next four chapters present strategies for innovations meeting various combinations of corporate and customer barriers, as organized by Figure 4.1 at the beginning of this chapter. The

---

*Our scores reflect our thinking and our experiences. One can expand the base of opinion by interviewing industry experts, corporate managers, and customers. Scientific research methods can improve the reliability of the scores.

TABLE 4.1
RATINGS OF CORPORATE CUSTOMER BARRIERS TO SELECTED TELECOMMUNICATIONS INNOVATIONS

Barriers	Videotex	ISDN	Electronic Mail	Lifeline Service	Digital Centrex	Cellular Mobile Phones	800-Number Service	Custom Calling Services
			Corporate					
Expertise	8	9	2	1	5	7	2	1
Operations	8	8	2	1	7	9	1	1
Resources	9	10	5	1	8	8	2	1
Regulation	5	5	2	1	5	3	2	1
Market Access	2	5	1	1	7	5	1	2
CORPORATE SUBTOTAL	32	37	12	5	32	32	8	6
			Customer					
Usage	9	9	7	6	2	2	2	1
Value	9	7	6	8	5	3	2	4
Risk	8	8	8	6	4	2	2	1
Tradition	5	8	8	6	2	1	1	1
Image	2	3	2	8	1	1	1	1
CUSTOMER SUBTOTAL	33	35	31	34	14	9	8	8
TOTAL SCORE	65	72	43	39	46	41	16	14

137

first option, discussed in chapter 5, addresses the needs of an innovation facing strong corporate and customer barriers.

McManus, K. "Wrong Numbers." *Forbes*, June 4, 1984, 154–155.

Tydeman, J., et. al. "Teletext and Videotext in the United States: Market Potential, Technology, Public Policy Issues." New York: McGraw-Hill Inc., 1982.

Wiener, N. "Should You Invest in Private Videotex?" *Business Marketing*, March 1984, 66–77.

"Videotex." *Advertising Age*, Nov. 16, 1981, Sec 2: S1-S23.

"Publishers Go Electronic." *Business Week*, June 11, 1984, 84–97.

"Videotex: Technology in Search of Markets." *Direct Marketing*, Oct. 1982, 88.

"Cutthroat Competition in Mobile Phones." *Fortune*, Feb. 6, 1984.

"Mobile Phones: Hot New Industry." *Fortune*, Aug. 6, 1984, 108–113.

Part 2
Breaking the Barriers

Our discussion in Part 1 emphasized two key points. First, the 1980s represent a new era for business firms, an era in which innovations will dictate corporate growth and profitability. The success of a firm will thus depend on the speed and ability with which it can adapt to new technologies while responding to customer needs.

Second, innovations tend to create a high degree of change or discontinuity for both the innovating firm and the intended customer. The higher the discontinuity for the firm, the higher the corporate barriers to the innovation, and the slower the product development process. The higher the discontinuity for the customer, the higher the market barriers to the innovation, and the slower the market development process.

Firms are thus confronted with a dilemma: Innovations are indispensable for survival, yet the high degree of change accompanying them is inevitable, too. Successfully innovating requires understanding and coping with the corporate and customer barriers to innovation. Four different strategies can be

	Customer barriers	
Corporate barriers	High	Low
High	"Slow and steady"	"Migrate and maintain"
Low	"Pick and protect"	"Grab and grow"

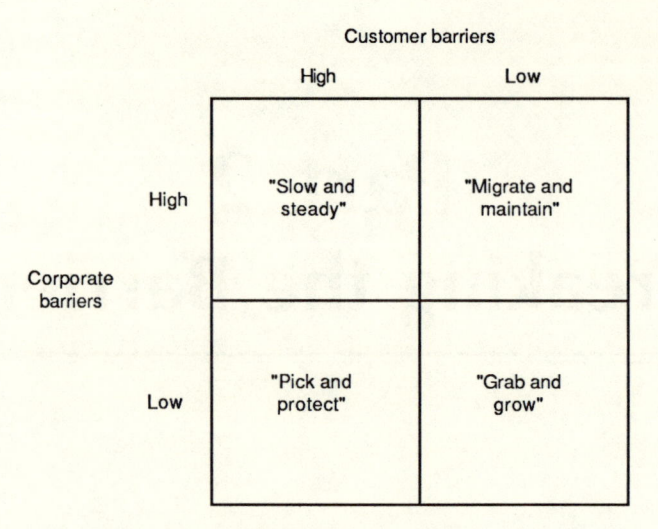

Figure II.1. Strategy matrix

used to break the barriers to innovation, as shown in the matrix in Figure II.1.

In this part, we will examine the rationale underlying each of these strategies and describe how they work effectively. One chapter has been devoted to the discussion of each strategy. Chapter 5 discusses the Slow and Steady strategy, which advocates cautious, purposeful progress when an innovation faces high corporate and customer barriers. Chapter 6 examines the Grab and Grow strategy, which suggests rapid appropriation of customers when both sets of barriers are low. Chapter 7 looks at the Pick and Protect strategy, which recommends being judicious about customer selection when customer barriers are high and corporate barriers low. Chapter 8 addresses how to retain customers when those conditions are reversed by using the Migrate and Maintain strategy.

5
The Slow and Steady Strategy

When an innovation runs up against high corporate barriers as well as high customer barriers, what we call the Slow and Steady (S&S) strategy is the right one to adopt (see Figure 5.1). In other words, this strategy is ideal when the firm is not structurally ready to offer the innovative product or service and the customer is not yet ready to adopt it.

The S&S strategy consists of introducing a product or service to the market on a very selective basis. Market development is conducted incrementally, starting with customers for whom the product provides the highest value, and sequentially moving to other customers for whom the product offers a significant but decreasing relative value. The S&S strategy thus accesses several layers of the market in slow but steady succession. The pricing strategy used for the innovation reflects this value progression. You charge the highest prices to the customers who most value the innovation, and from there on you adjust prices to correspond to the descending customer interest (see Figure 5.2).

IBM Adopted this strategy successfully when they introduced

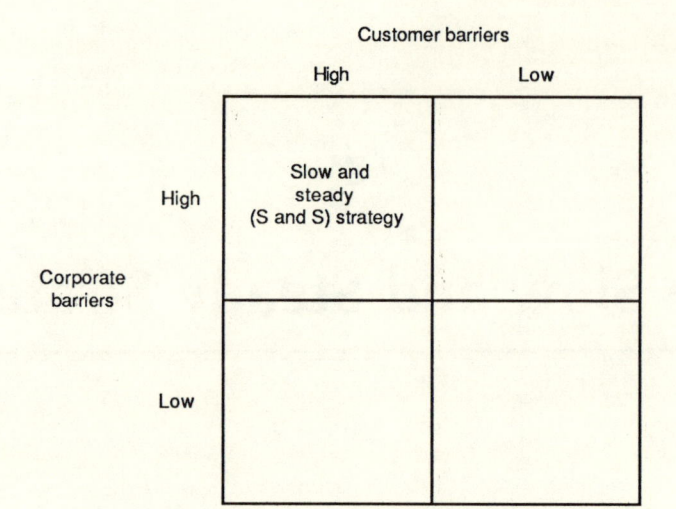

Figure 5.1. Strategy matrix: Slow and Steady

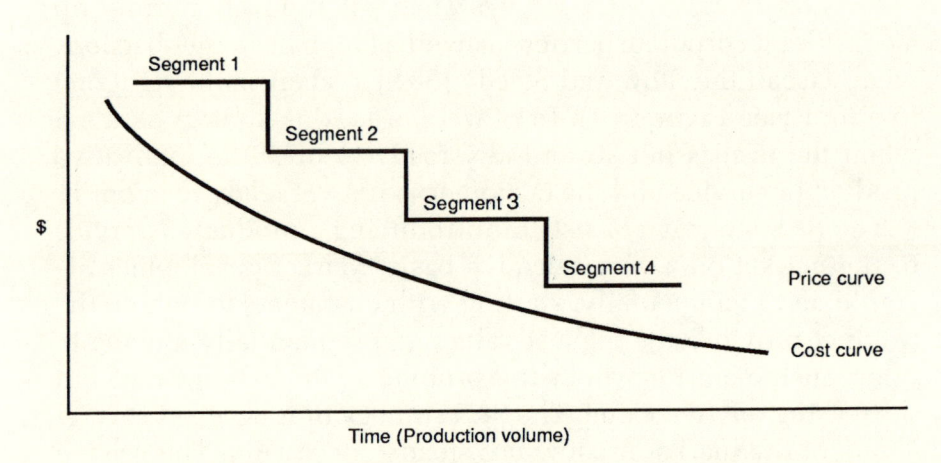

Figure 5.2. Pricing mechanism for the Slow and Steady strategy

The Slow and Steady Strategy

their first mainframe computer. The product was totally new to IBM and created high corporate discontinuity. IBM was then primarily in the typewriter business, using old electromechanical technology. To produce computers, they had to get into the electronics business, which necessitated a heavy investment in expertise and production facilities. Besides expanding plant capacity, IBM had to develop a totally new computer operating language as well as a new user language (FORTRAN). The latter alone took nearly a decade.

The product was also totally new to the customers, thus creating uneasiness on that side. No one knew how to operate a mainframe computer system. In fact, the very term *computer* was foreign. Even the concept was disturbing. The anxiety of the time was that the new thinking machines would replace and control humans. And, in a functional sense, computers were truly disruptive because they required a reorganization of the work flow.

Further, customers were forced to learn how to use the mainframes and to continually improve their skills over time. As a result, they threw up a high usage barrier. Also, the high purchase cost combined with a new, unsure product created economic risk and performance uncertainty barriers since not all customers were sure whether the mainframe would justify the investment.

Given this situation, IBM rightly chose to proceed at a slow and steady pace at first. They decided to go after the Fortune 500 companies and government agencies, which stood to gain the most from cost efficiencies in data handling. This segment of the market could afford the higher introductory price of the product and could justify the cost on the basis of the tremendous *value* gained. Only after IBM had catered to the needs of government and big business did they make a gradual entry into the mid-sized segment—and much later into the small-sized segment (see Figure 5.3).

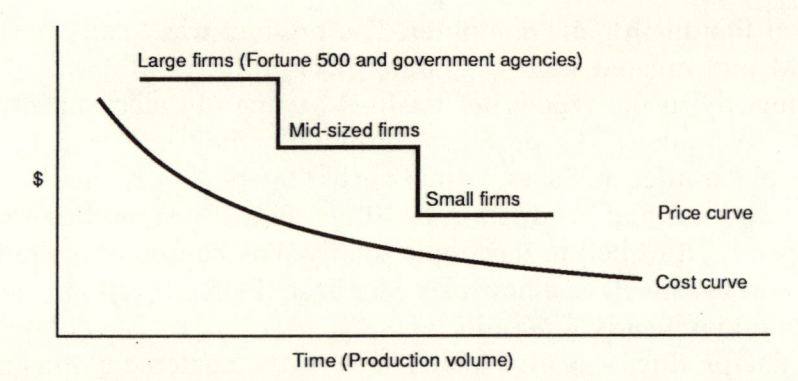

Figure 5.3. IBM's pricing approach for the mainframe computer using the Slow and Steady strategy

STRATEGIC OCCASIONS

The S&S strategy can be used successfully if there are high corporate barriers and high customer barriers for the innovation.

These conditions occur in a number of instances throughout our economy: in capital goods and industrial supplies, and in a wide range of consumer goods and services. We will first look at several situations in which the occasion merited the S&S strategy. In the next section we will then describe how this strategy was successfully applied in each case.

Situation 1: A Steal over Steel

The innovative material, Kevlar, encountered both high corporate discontinuity and high customer discontinuity when it was introduced a generation ago by DuPont. First, any innovation or technology based on chemistry is inherently more difficult and less predictable. In developing Kevlar as a chemical substitute for steel, DuPont could not borrow from their prior experiences from their other successful materials (nylon, dacron, and polyester). DuPont had to organize a separate team of scientists to work on the development of Kevlar. They diverted a part of their talented R&D personnel into the development of a product whose payoff was not guaranteed.

Second, DuPont had to build a separate manufacturing facility for Kevlar. The existing chemical processing plants could not be utilized because Kevlar was totally different in formulation and processing. DuPont had to invest nearly $250 million to develop and produce limited amounts of the product in 1965. Third, since it was a new chemical, there were also many regulatory uncertainties. It had to be properly tested and certified to ensure that there were no unhealthy side effects in the production, distribution, usage, and disposal of Kevlar.

From the customer's perspective, Kevlar was a radically new product. Airplane manufacturers, to note just one large user, which had relied on steel and aluminum for all their history, were now faced with considering a chemical fiber as a feasible substitute. The product, of course, had no prior record in similar applications. Performance uncertainty was, consequently, very high. Steel customers were equally unsure whether Kevlar could completely replace steel or whether only a partial replacement could be effected. Thus, there was also a usage barrier because their whole pattern of acquisition, storage, and assembly was threatened. Machines designed to bend steel were, for instance, inappropriate for forming Kevlar.

Situation 2: Publish or Perish

Electronic publishing—electronically producing, processing, storing, printing, and retrieving information—is a classic example of an innovation that has had to overcome high barriers from both the corporate side and the customer side. Traditionally, the publishing industry has relied on printing technology. But, with the explosion of information processing technology, especially using computers and video, the industry has been exposed to tremendous structural innovation.

The new technology has imposed a number of changes on the publishers and, consequently, has had to reckon with the structural barriers that publishers have erected. First, there are operational changes. Any company switching to the new technology has been forced to invest in new operational facilities. The printing press is becoming a thing of the past, an obsolete piece of machinery. What is needed is computer hardware and software. New equipment requires, in turn, learning a new mode of operation.

Second, there are major resource expenditures in the purchase of new computer equipment. While traditional publishing has been labor-intensive, electronic publishing is capital-intensive and requires enormous amounts of capital up front.

Third, electronic publishing faces major expertise barriers. Corporations have had to acquire new editorial and management skills to make their investments pay off. For example, because of the switch in information delivery from print to computer terminals, newswriters and editors have had to learn to write paragraphs that do not exceed the 25 lines that a typical computer screen could display. Further, publishers have also had to become much more familiar with electronic technology than ever before, just to keep ahead of the competition in terms of seizing market opportunities and cutting costs. Further, the planning horizon for machinery has dropped to a period of 6 to 12 months, thanks to the rapid development of electronic technology. Printing technology had afforded them the luxury of two or even three years for planning; now publishers must upgrade machinery sooner and more often.

Finally, electronic publishers have had to overcome market access barriers. They have had to develop their own mode of access to the readers and distributors of printed material through computer telecommunications networks, another expensive and time-consuming process.

Electronic publishing is thus an innovation facing high structural resistance, even from corporations that want to implement it. The innovation is also confronted with customer barriers.

The average reader of printed information has been forced to drastically alter his or her usage patterns. Obtaining electronic news is not as easy as opening a newspaper or relaxing in an armchair and watching television. The customer needs a computer terminal to start with, and this requires a major capital expenditure. Further, he or she has to pay a regular fee to access the news service. He or she also has to learn how to use the computerized information system. The customer is thus faced with spending more money and effort for getting the same information, by no means an alluring prospect!

Situation 3: An Emission by Any Other Name...

The microwave oven made its shaky debut into the marketplace in the late 1960s—faced with stiff corporate and customer barriers.

The manufacture of microwave ovens required a totally different know-how from that needed for making traditional convection ovens. The first corporate barrier was thus an expertise deficiency; microwave technology was not invented by an appliance company. Second, companies had to consider investing in totally new production facilities, which simultaneously imposed operational and resource barriers. Finally, there were regulatory problems, because microwave radiation was still under government evaluation.

The microwave oven also had to reckon with problems on the customer's end. The customers knew full well that microwave technology was based on irradiation; that is, it heated foods by radiation, unlike the safe traditional ovens, which used electricity or natural gas. How could radiation be safe after what happened at Hiroshima? Radiation technology thus created an image barrier as well as a performance uncertainty (risk) barrier. Microwaves also disrupted usage patterns because different cooking skills and dishes were required. The food didn't always taste the same, either. There were, in sum, a lot of differences to overcome for the sake of speed.

Situation 4: Hard to Swallow!

When oral contraceptives were first invented, they were hailed as a great technological breakthrough. Prior to the pill, birth control devices were mostly mechanical (IUD, condom) or surgical (vasectomy or ligation). As a pharmaceutical product, the pill also required totally different production and packaging facilities. There were significant regulatory barriers as well, especially as they related to reliability, side effects, and long-term ramifications of taking the pill. Finally, there were strong market access barriers created by religious attitudes of people about birth control in general.

From customers in developed countries (such as the United States), the product faced usage barriers and risk barriers. Potential customers were unaccustomed to the regimen of taking a pill every day and were uncertain about its effectiveness. They also worried about long-term effects on their health. From customers in developing countries (such as in the Third World), the product faced an entirely different kind of barrier: a negative image. The less well-educated and the less literate people associated pills with medicines to cure headaches and body aches. They couldn't believe that anything consumed like a headache remedy could prevent pregnancy! For women in all societies there was a challenge to the traditional valuing of motherhood that daily birth control seemed to flaunt on a regular basis.

STRATEGIC VARIATIONS

We have four unique occasions in which an innovation was impeded by high corporate and customer barriers. Each, however,

Strategic Variations

was marketable using the Slow and Steady strategy. DuPont's introduction of Kevlar illustrates this process perfectly.

The New Fiber Steps Out

A company using the S&S strategy must first list, in order of priority, the customer needs for the product and then serve the market in that order.

Lighter than Steel. Kevlar was originally developed to replace steel wire in the belts of radial tires of automobiles. The market segment that found the innovation most attractive, however, was the aircraft industry. Kevlar gained acceptance as a plastic reinforcement of fiberglass. It had superior durability and could withstand impacts better than steel. It had good electrical and chemical resistance as well, could reduce vibrations, and even improve the aesthetics of the plane. Above all, the greatest advantage of using Kevlar in aerospace and commercial aircraft industries was its light weight—always a key consideration, because it takes three pounds of aircraft fuel to raise one pound of payload off the ground. In spacecraft, this ratio increases tremendously to 20:1. Every pound of heavier material that can be taken out of an airplane and replaced by Kevlar saves the carrier as much as $300 in fuel over the life of the plane. Lockheed was the first commercial aircraft user of Kevlar when it put 1300 pounds of the fiber in its L-1011. Today, the DC-10, the deHavilland DHC-7, and the Sikorsky-76 helicopter contain Kevlar, and the Boeing 757 and Boeing 767 are expected to incorporate Kevlar in large quantities.

The first step of DuPont's S&S strategy, therefore, was to develop the product for the airplane industry (see Figure 5.4). The company then focused its attention on the market for body armor.

Taking Armed Protection Lightly. Police forces throughout the United States buy bulletproof vests to protect their officers from

150 The Slow and Steady Strategy

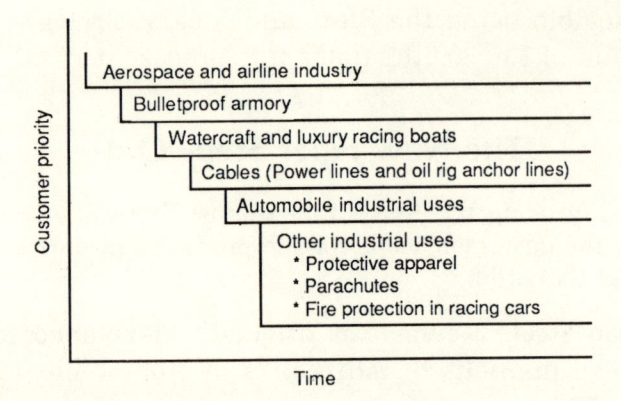

```
Customer priority ^
  | Aerospace and airline industry
  |   Bulletproof armory
  |     Watercraft and luxury racing boats
  |       Cables (Power lines and oil rig anchor lines)
  |         Automobile industrial uses
  |           Other industrial uses
  |             * Protective apparel
  |             * Parachutes
  |             * Fire protection in racing cars
  +------------------------------------> Time
```

Figure 5.4. Time sequence of market development for Kevlar

serious injury or death. The amount of protection offered by a vest depends upon the amount of tough material that it contains. Kevlar is as tough as steel. In general, a vest made with eight layers of Kevlar can protect the wearer from most handgun threats, including .38 specials, .45 automatics, and .357 magnums. Such a vest weighs only 1.5 to 3 pounds. Additional layers are needed to protect against higher caliber handguns. For instance, a vest of 23 layers is required to stop 9mm. machine-gun rounds and even .45 caliber magnum bullets. Naturally, this vest is bulkier and costs more.

Nylon has been used in flexible body armor. A vest of Kevlar, however, weighs 50 percent less and provides the same protection. As an added value, Kevlar vests can be outfitted with an impact-resistant plastic to dissipate the bullet's tendency to leave severe bruises. The U.S. Army has also approved Kevlar helmets to replace steel helmets, since Kevlar helmets provide increased fragment protection at essentially the same weight. Lightweight armor was also installed on the U.S. Navy's guided missile frigates to provide protection for critical areas without adding excess weight. Similar protection systems have been built for assault helicopters and armored vehicles.

Armored protection offered by Kevlar is available in nonmilitary areas as well. For instance, lightweight, bulletproof vests are very popular among executives. The vests are tailored so that they can be worn with ordinary suits. Depending upon the type of protection required, a vest can cost anywhere from $300 to $1500. Beside vests, there are also bulletproof raincoat liners, jackets, umbrellas, camera cases, clipboards, and briefcases.

Thus, the second segment of the market developed by Kevlar was the soft and hard armor market. The S&S strategy was well on its way.

Hotter on Water. The next lucrative market for Kevlar was watercraft. Canoes and kayaks were the first to incorporate Kevlar into construction. Power boats soon followed. Fishing and performance boats with Kevlar-reinforced hulls weighed at least 20 percent less than fiberglass and could go much faster with the same-power engines. In other words, the same performance was obtained with less horsepower, with the added advantages of higher speed and less spent fuel. An increasing number of luxury racing boats were also fitted with masts reinforced with Kevlar. Because they were lighter, these masts had less drag than conventional masts; hence, racing boats so outfitted could reach speeds in excess of 90 miles-per-hour and do consistently well in races. Slowly but surely, Kevlar had captured a third lucrative market segment.

High Wire. Kevlar's next target market was ropes and cables. Ropes made with Kevlar have about twice the strength of nylon or polyester ropes of equal weight, and about the same strength as steel wire ropes at just one-fourth the weight. This high strength-to-weight ratio is of great value in the construction of power transmission lines. The copper-aluminum wires used for

```
Transmission lines
shielded by steel

Transmission lines
shielded by kevlar
```

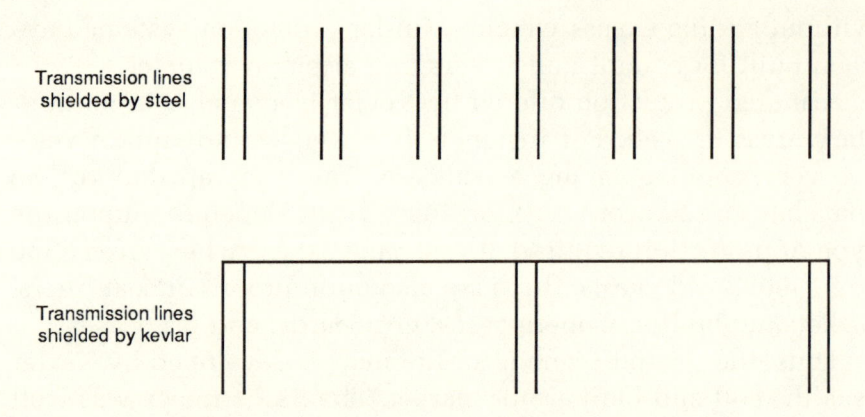

Figure 5.5. Kevlar vs. steel transmission lines

carrying electricity are usually shielded by steel. Wooden poles are normally provided as supports for these electric wires. Steel, being quite heavy, has an innate tendency to sag; hence, many more poles are required to support wires shielded by steel rather than those supported by Kevlar (see Figure 5.5).

Using Kevlar in place of steel thus minimizes the number of wooden poles required as supports. In flat terrain, such as in the Midwest, wooden poles are easy to transport and install. So, using Kevlar in electric cables provides no special advantage. However, in rough, uneven terrain, as in the Rocky Mountain states, the story is different. Transportation of both the poles and the installation crews is very expensive because men and materials must be moved by helicopter. The costs of operations are very high, and the job is extremely cumbersome. Every installation avoided represents a tremendous saving, and Kevlar offers this benefit.

Once again, Kevlar has made its entry into another lucrative market segment—using the S&S approach.

Oil Drilling No Longer a Rigamarole. Another application for which Kevlar has replaced steel is in the manufacture of pendant lines to anchor offshore oil drilling rigs. As oil-site exploration went into deeper waters, the steel wire cable for rig-anchoring systems reached its limits, due to steel's low strength-to-weight ratio. The pendant lines have to support a 30,000 pound anchor as it is being placed into position by a work boat. They also must withstand the extreme lifting forces required to dislodge the anchor upon retrieval. While the oil rig is in place, the pendant is supported by a buoy, which must have sufficient flotation to suspend the weight. A typical drilling rig is moved four times a year and requires the retrieval and deployment of eight anchors. A great deal of time is required to coil and handle heavy and cumbersome steel pendant lines. Tests in the field showed that using Kevlar ropes could reduce retrieval and deployment time by 25 percent. Furthermore, pendant lines made of Kevlar allow a lighter, smaller, and less costly buoy. The tremendous savings in capital and operational costs provided by Kevlar make it the logical successor for steel in pendant lines.

A Strong Grip on the Tire Market. The next market that Kevlar pursued was, ironically, the market for which it had been groomed: the replacement of steel wire in the belts of radial tires. Steel adds to the dead weight of automobiles. Kevlar-made tires, on the other hand, are considerably lighter and thus increase the fuel efficiency of cars. Because Kevlar is more flexible than steel, it improves riding comfort and reduces the noise level. Due to its better energy absorption properties, Kevlar also generates less heat buildup. It is also unaffected by moisture accumulation in the tires. All of this leads to better wearing tires and improved blowout protection.

The Goodyear tire company took note of the advantages of the fiber and decided in the early 1980s to play a pioneering role (as an original equipment manufacturer) in its use for beltings for radial tires. Today, no less than seven major tire companies are marketing radial tires with Kevlar belts.

And on to Glory. Once the utility of Kevlar had been established in airline construction, bulletproof clothing, boats, power cables, and automobile tires, it spread like wildfire to other markets. It has, for instance, replaced conventional materials such as fiberglass, polyester, nylon, rayon, and steel wire in automobile hoses and V-belts, in power transmission belts for both vehicles and machinery, in snowmobile belts, and in high-pressure hoses that carry hot liquids and corrosive materials.

Kevlar has gained acceptance in the manufacture of (nonballistic) protective apparel. Kevlar gloves are used in the metals- and glass-handling industries in place of cotton. With the same degree of comfort and dexterity as cotton, Kevlar gloves offer twice the cut resistance and better wear.

Leggings made of Kevlar are used to protect lumbermen from chainsaw injuries. Industrial gloves made of Kevlar are increasingly worn where people need protection from heat or cold. Kevlar offers better abrasion resistance and longer life than asbestos gloves, and it also protects at temperatures as high as 800 degrees to 1000 degrees Fahrenheit.

Kevlar has been used to develop fuel cell systems for added protection against fires in racing cars, such as Lotus and Tiger (Formula 1 racers), as well as in non-Formula 1 cars such as the BMW. The U.S. military has adopted uncoated Kevlar for use in lightweight parachutes, aircraft ejection seats, and ballistic missile deceleration.

The lesson here is that the Slow and Steady strategy works. DuPont succeeded with Kevlar once the company developed applications based on customer priority and entered the market for each application in its turn.

The Other Cases

Electronic publishing has been similarly groomed for success by focusing on those applications for which it provides the great-

Strategic Variations

est value. The major advantage of electronic news, as compared to newspapers and television, is its time value. The news can be constantly updated and made available to those who need current information every minute of the day. For example, stock brokerage services are now able to keep pace with market developments from the start until the finish of trading each business day. The availability of financial information at the moment a decision has to be made means a savings of several thousands of dollars—which more than justifies subscribing to the electronic news.

The publishers of *USA Today*, the *Wall Street Journal*, the *New York Times*, and others are also convinced of the need to make at least a partial switch to electronic technology. It provides a cost-effective way of storing old information. No longer is it necessary to physically preserve back issues of a periodical, because disk space on the computer performs this function quite well. Electronic technology also allows faster conversations between publishers who borrow news from each other. Thus, several publishers can justify a partial, if not a full-fledged, investment in electronic technology. In this way, the innovation can make a slow, steady progress in the marketplace.

Makers of microwave ovens began to break the barriers systematically. First of all, they aligned with prepared foods companies and fast food restaurants to ensure that microwave ovens and foods were compatible. They perfected the technology to ensure there were virtually no radiation leaks, especially through the front glass. They started educational programs in home economics classes to encourage future homemakers to learn how to use microwave ovens. Finally, the cost of microwaves began to come down as the industry's production capacity increased, making the product more affordable to the masses. They also redesigned microwave ovens with electronic controls so that users had much less to learn.

When oral contraceptives were introduced in the Third World

countries, the S&S strategy also worked quite well. The effectiveness of the pill was first conveyed to urban factory and clerical workers, who had at least a high school education. This group was more receptive to the idea of daily oral contraception and realized the value of the product. Once there was acceptance among this segment, and the performance of oral contraceptives was established, favorable word-of-mouth advertising and testimonials trickled to the less educated, more resistant groups of people. In the United States and other developed countries, the pill was also targeted at the educated population but limited to career-oriented families where the wife was more interested in being a breadwinner than a homemaker. The ultimate market acceptance was thus generated by a slow, steady process.

STRATEGIC CONDITIONS

Entry Barriers

For the Slow and Steady strategy to be successful, a company must be certain that it is protected by high entry barriers. If competitive entry cannot be delayed, a firm cannot risk the luxury of slow market development.

It took DuPont years of research and nearly $250 million of capital investment to develop the first generation of Kevlar in 1965. It took five more years of testing and modification to arrive at a product that could be commercialized. Once DuPont had developed the proprietary technology, it invested an additional $250 million in a production plant in Richmond, Virginia. These vast amounts of resources invested in developing, testing, and commercializing the product proved to be a deterrent to any competitor who contemplated entering the industry.

Strategic Conditions

Furthermore, the DuPont research team consisted of experts who specialized in the development of synthetic fibers with unique properties. The earlier success of nylon, a revolutionary material, bears testimony to their technical expertise. This unique reserve of expertise gives DuPont an edge over its competitors.

Finally, DuPont has always guarded its technological breakthroughs with patent protection, thus gaining sufficient time to entrench itself in the market. Armed with these entry barriers—resources, technical expertise, and patent protection—DuPont employed the S&S strategy to launch Kevlar on a successful voyage.

IBM also had the advantage of high entry barriers when it came out with the first mainframe computer. The company's R&D competence, as well as IBM's high amounts of capital investment, contributed to a tremendous edge over potential competitors. Customers felt safe with Big Blue, and competitors found it difficult to overcome customer inertia to switch to other brands, even after investing heavily to produce a state-of-the-art product. IBM's after-sales service created a high degree of customer loyalty, which proved to be the most effective barrier to competitive entry. IBM was thus able to establish supremacy in the market at its own pace.

In electronic publishing, Knight-Ridder Services has built up a tremendous competitive advantage by heavily investing in electronic technology. It is thus protected from competitive onslaught by the twin barriers of financial resources and technological sophistication. Similarly, in the videotex market, AT&T enjoys access to both telecommunication technology and computer technology. Only IBM with its own acquisition of telecommunications technology poses a viable threat to AT&T.

The central point of all these illustrations is: Once you are on the other side of the barrier, it works for you against potential competitors.

Cost Recovery

The S&S strategy is designed to allow quick recovery of the high costs of production and R&D for the innovation.

According to the study conducted by Booz, Allen & Hamilton in 1982, the costs of R&D and production that are associated with new product marketing have been increasing rapidly. Commercialization costs for exploration, screening, business analysis, and product development are 75 percent (as against 50 percent in 1958) of the total expenditures incurred in marketing a new product. Given this scenario, cost recovery has become an important consideration in new product development. The S&S strategy facilitates frugality by targeting the product initially at the most lucrative segments, thus maximizing profitability.

Let's consider a few representative cases. When, for instance, personal computers were first introduced to the market in 1977, Tandy Corporation was one of the early entrants. Tandy Corporation sold the product through its own Radio Shack outlets; even the least expensive version of its TRS 80 model retailed at $600. This high price was intended to provide cost recovery, since those customers who placed a high value on the product would be willing to pay more for it.

That was how television crept into our lives. When televisions were first introduced, the unit price of each set was substantially higher than in later years, after market penetration. Again, the reason was cost recovery. Similarly, air bags are being built into the higher priced automobiles first, to ease market adoption among the less price-sensitive segments and to ensure cost recovery.

Cable communications made a successful debut into television programming by catering to customers who were willing to pay an additional subscription fee. For example, in rural communities, cable was a cost-effective medium, since about 200 individuals to every mile shared the costs of setting up the transmission tower. Further, several customers were eager to

Strategic Conditions

subscribe to first-run movies on special-purpose channels such as HBO. Other specialized programming such as health (Cable Health Network), entertainment for ethnic groups (Black Entertainment Television), sports (ESPN), and adult entertainment (Playboy channel) generated high customer interest and sufficient revenues to recover the costs of initial setup and development.

Finally, DuPont's S&S strategy for Kevlar also ensured rapid recovery of costs. The aircraft industry and the armor market represented the highest profit potential. They let Kevlar in and paid DuPont back at the same time.

Unique Technology

If the innovation is based on a new technology, customers are not in a position to evaluate its performance against an equivalent substitute.

Think back to the beginning of the Xerox revolution. Their first copier machine was unique, a real breakthrough. At that time, no other product in the market bore even a remote resemblance to it. Customers were favorably impressed by the absolute performance level of the innovation. Yet, they were unable to make an accurate estimate of the true value of the product, since they could not compare it to anything similar. They bought it because it had a real, discoverable value.

Similarly, when DuPont introduced Kevlar, it was the only one on the market and so automatically became the industry standard. No other company had access to the technology. Comparisons could be made with only the not-so-similar substitutes: steel, fiberglass, and asbestos. Firms that used those substitutes in large quantities were willing to pay a premium to switch to the new fiber because of its special properties.

When vasectomy was introduced as a method of birth control, it was the first permanent contraception method aimed at the male. The method assured absolute safety and virtually eliminated risk of pregnancy. Some men, however, associated the process with loss of manhood and were thus strongly against it. But there were others who believed in the effectiveness of the method, even though a fair assessment of its value (as compared to a contraceptive method for women) could not be made. As more men tried the procedure, news of its acceptability spread slowly and steadily. Today, vasectomies are becoming more and more common.

Finally, Procter & Gamble's success with Pampers disposable diapers was based on the uniqueness of the product. The disposable diaper had a pad with a special pleat for a better fit, was absorbent, and could be thrown away. The pad was inserted into pants that contained a newly invented, thin sheet of plastic across the back. This construction kept the moisture in, but allowed the circulation of air, which was necessary in hot, humid places. Another feature—a porous sheet between the baby and the absorbent material—allowed the fluid to pass through to the diaper but prevented most of it from coming back through again, kept the babies drier and more comfortable, and justified the product's advertising theme: "America's number one alternative to a wet bottom." To housewives, who were used to cloth diapers and a never-ending laundry load, the disposable diaper was a unique product. Since there was nothing equivalent on the market, a cost comparison was not possible. But the diapers guaranteed dryness for the baby as well as easy disposal after usage, and mothers were only too willing to buy them.

Leading-Edge Marketing

The firm that uses the S&S strategy should always commence with the leading edge of the market.

In the corporate world, the leading-edge customers are the firms with sophisticated technology, generally the *Fortune* 500 companies. For example, Satellite Business Communications (SBS)—jointly owned at that time by IBM, Aetna Life and Casualty Company, and the COMSAT General Corporation—developed a new technology designed to provide high-speed, high-capacity data transport over long distances. These private data networks operated using satellites and earth stations. Since they featured wide band channels, they could handle switch-data transmission, video teleconferencing, and electronic mail, as well as standard voice communications. In contrast, narrow band channels allow voice transmissions only.

SBS (now owned by MCI) has targeted its service at the *Fortune* 500 companies. Since these corporations have high geographic dispersion, they stand to benefit the most from the advanced data networks. These firms also have the highest buying power. SBS is thus hoping to follow the path taken by other technological innovations such as computers, ride the initial impetus provided by the adoption of leading-edge firms, and slowly and steadily build the foundation for market success.

For consumer products and services, the leading-edge customers are the opinion leaders: the young, affluent, educated and mobile individuals who have both the willingness to try something new and the ability to pay for it. When personal computers were first introduced into the consumer market, the affluent home-users contributed to the PC's success. The buyers were rich professionals who used PCs for their hobbies or to automate home accounts. Once they realized the value of the innovation, they brought it into their workplace and ignited the rapid growth of personal computers.

CAVEATS

Before you decide to use the Slow and Steady strategy, be absolutely sure that (1) there are a sufficient number of customers with high usage potential for the new product or service and

(2) the customers are willing to pay a higher price for your new offering. Unless these two conditions are met, the strategy can backfire and become a long-drawn-out hassle for your firm.

The tale of lead free gasoline illustrates the dangers of abusing the S&S strategy. Standard Oil Company of Indiana observed that several automobile engines suffered from the problem of knocking. In response, they invested millions of dollars to develop a refining process that would produce lead free gasoline with antiknocking properties. The company successfully developed the new product and decided that a good distribution network was all that was required to effectively market it. Accordingly, in the early 1970s, Standard Oil acquired trucks to transport the lead free gas and dedicated service stations to pump it to the cars of eagerly waiting customers.

Unfortunately, the thoroughness with which the company planned its moves hardly matched the outcome. The market was not ready for the product. The benefits of using lead free gas were not evident to the customers, and once they could see no additional value, they couldn't justify paying the higher price charged by the company to recoup costs.

Standard Oil first positioned the product as environmentally sound because it cut lead emissions into the atmosphere. Johnny Cash was enlisted to promote the ecological benefits of the gasoline. When this effort failed to make a significant impact, the company gradually lowered the price until it matched that of regular gas. Still, there was no sign of enthusiasm in the market. The major problem, of course, was that 9 out of 10 car engines were not designed to receive lead free gas, and thus only a small fraction of the market was open.

At this time, however, the Environmental Protection Agency (EPA) became more and more concerned with the lead content in the exhaust fumes of automobiles. Under increasing social and political pressure to rectify the problem, the EPA mandated that automobiles manufactured after 1974 be designed to use only unleaded gasoline. It was only after the government acted that the demand for lead free gas jumped. The market was finally ready for the product.

The S&S strategy thus fails when the innovation pursues a market that is not yet ready for it. While embracing a new technology is important for any firm, the firm cannot lose sight of customer needs if it wants to succeed. The customers did not perceive that the antiknocking properties of lead free gasoline provided any great benefit until the government mandated its use in new cars. When approached correctly, however, and when all conditions are ripe, the Slow and Steady strategy can overcome even the combination of high barriers erected both by the corporate structure and by customer behavior patterns.

SUMMARY

The Slow and Steady strategy is the correct response when the corporation is not structurally ready to offer the innovative product or service and the customer is not yet ready to adopt it. The product or service is introduced to the market on a very selective basis, starting with customers who value it the most and then moving on to others for whom the relative value is progressively less. Pricing reflects both the declining customer value and the declining costs to the firm as it gains experience in production.

Kevlar as a substitute for steel, electronic publishing, microwave ovens, and oral contraceptives were all innovative offerings that faced high corporate and high customer barriers on their way to market. Each was able, however, to succeed in the marketplace by proceeding at a slow and steady pace.

Slow market development requires that the innovative firm be protected from competition by high entry barriers. The S&S strategy does, however, allow quick recovery of the high costs of R&D and production. If the technology is new, customers will have trouble evaluating it. Firms should begin their marketing efforts, therefore, with leading-edge customers. Ultimately, the

S&S strategy will work only if there are enough customers with high usage potential who are willing to pay a higher price.

The Slow and Steady approach is appropriate when conditions are at their worst: high corporate and customer barriers. We will next consider a strategy (Grab and Grow) that should be used when the opposite conditions occur: when both sets of barriers are low.

Flanagan, W.G. "Arms and the Man." *Forbes*, July 6, 1981, 36.

Lowndes, J.C. "New Blade Containment Saves Weight." *Aviation Week & Space Technology*, May 18, 1981, 33.

McCann, M.K. "Fibre Finds Automotive Applications." *Automotive Industry*, Feb. 1981, 47–48.

Seidel, L.E. "Many Uses of Kevlar Aramid." *Textile Industry*, March 1981, 48–49.

"Cable TV." *Advertising Age*, April 26, 1982, Sec 2:M11-M37.

"Discovering a Vast Potential Market." *Business Week*, June 23, 1980, 125.

"DuPont Aims Kevlar at New Markets." *Chemical Week*, Nov 26, 1980.

"Market for Cable TV." *Business*, July-Aug.-Sept. 1982, 54.

"Miracle in Search of a Market." *Fortune*, Dec. 1, 1980, 92–98.

"MTV Draws Millions to a New Medium." *SMM*, Jan. 17, 1983, 32.

"State of the Industry, 1982: The Cable Conection." *Broadcasting*, May 3, 1982, 37–70.

6
The Grab and Grow Strategy

When an innovation faces the enviable situation of low corporate barriers and low customer barriers, it is time to take advantage and employ what we call the Grab and Grow strategy (see Figure 6.1). Grab and Grow (G&G) works well when the firm is structurally ready to produce the innovation and the market is ready to use it.

The Grab and Grow strategy entails introducing the innovation on a mass market basis. The firm intends to produce the innovation for the large number of customers who are ready for it and thus capitalize on the product/service's early entry into the market. Early entry gives the firm an advantage over its competitors. The innovating firm builds its experience faster than its competitors and is thus able to obtain higher cost efficiency. The goal is to grab as much of the market as possible and grow rapidly into a formidable competitive position.

The pricing mechanism used by the G&G strategy is *not* geared to an intuitive cost-plus-margin system. Instead, it is based on anticipated increases in production volume and the consequent

The Grab and Grow Strategy

```
                    Customer barriers
              High                    Low
         ┌──────────────┬──────────────┐
         │              │              │
    High │              │              │
         │              │              │
Corporate├──────────────┼──────────────┤
barriers │              │              │
         │              │ Grab and grow│
     Low │              │ (G and G) strategy│
         │              │              │
         └──────────────┴──────────────┘
```

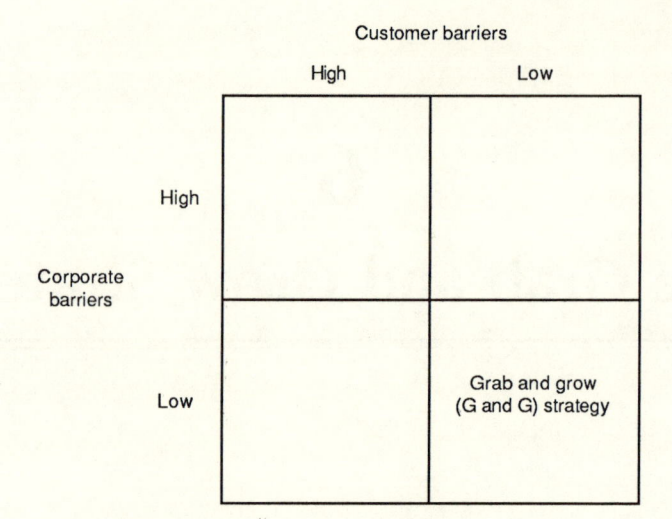

Figure 6.1. Strategy matrix: Grab and Grow

decline in production costs (see Figure 6.2). The innovating firm thus maintains a constant price right from the start. Initially, the price is well below the cost of the product, but the company is willing to absorb the initial loss to build a strong customer base and to entrench itself in the market. The low price also makes it risky and unprofitable for competitors to contemplate placing their own entries in the market. Once the firm reaches the break-even production volume, it begins to enjoy the fruits of its foresight. Sacrificing short-term profits in the interest of long-term gains in market share and profitability is the key principle underlying the Grab and Grow strategy.

The early success enjoyed by U.S. and Japanese firms in the digital watch market is primarily due to this effective pricing strategy. The possibility of making the digital watch attracted a group of aggressive U.S. and Japanese semiconductor manufacturers to the watch industry. Digital watches had no moving parts, so there was little wear and tear, and hardly any servicing or repair would be required. Further, these watches could

The Grab and Grow Strategy

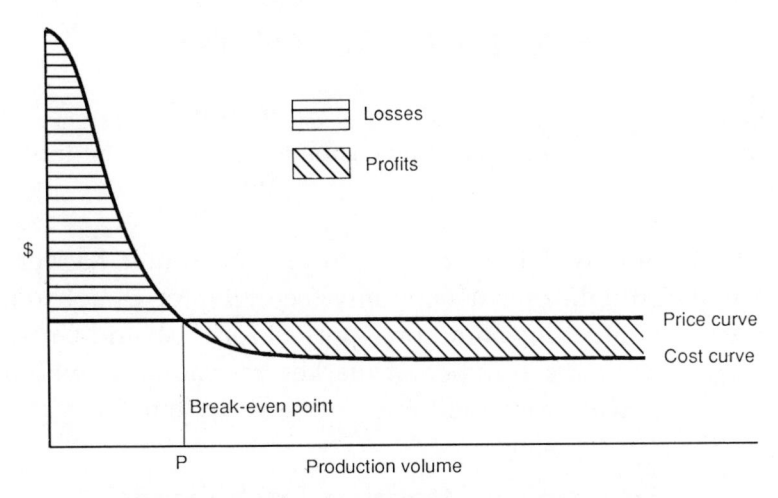

Figure 6.2. Pricing for the Grab and Grow strategy

be manufactured at costs far less than mechanical watches by squeezing more electronic circuitry into the design and eliminating several mechanical components. With increasing production volume, the firms improved their production efficiency, and the learning enjoyed by the firms helped decrease the costs still further. While the Swiss (mechanical) watchmakers were speculating on what to do, the U.S. and especially the Japanese electronic firms solved their teething problems, hired product designers and marketing specialists, and integrated their production facilities. Within two years, the unit price of digital watches was as low as $20, way below that of a Swiss watch. By displacing the mechanical watch, U.S. and Japanese firms took a strong hold of the watch market, *grabbing* customers for the digital watch and rapidly *growing* because of the price advantage.

Today, Casio, Seiko, and Citizen (all Japanese) dominate the watch business. Timex and Texas Instruments are not the major players they once were.

STRATEGIC OCCASIONS

The G&G strategy can be used successfully if there are very low corporate barriers and very low customer barriers to the innovation.

Just as combined high corporate and customer barriers are prevalent throughout our economy (see chapter 5) so, too, are the reverse conditions common—perfect for Grab and Grow. We will again look at a number of market occasions in which the G&G strategy was warranted and successfully employed.

Situation 1: Dashing Dashboards!

Chrysler Corporation plans to produce 200,000 subcompact cars with factory-installed radios. All the sound systems will be AM/FM stereophonic; no AM mono systems will be available. Capacity has already been increased at the Chrysler Huntsville electronics plant in Alabama to gear up for this deluge of subcompact H-body chassis. For Chrysler Corporation, this was a mere extension of earlier moves to master dashboard electronics. For example, Chrysler's entire 1984 model year sound-system line had electronically tuned radios (ETR) with clocks. No manually tuned systems were provided, and the ETRs were offered as deluxe options in all Chrysler products except the New Yorker. For their 1985 model year, Chrysler incorporated AM/FM stereo radio into their cassette players. For a company with automobile know-how and electronics know-how, producing cars equipped with stereo systems generated few problems. There were no operational, resource, or expertise barriers.

Customers did not construct any barriers to the innovative dashboards, either. Higher quality sound systems as a part of the manufacturer's original design and options package saved a lot of time and trouble for car buyers. Customers no longer had to look for the right system that would be compatible with the dashboard of their car. Nor did they have to worry about installing and servicing the system, since Chrysler would now take care of these details. Customers thus faced little risk in going for the factory-installed sound systems. Nor were any usage patterns disrupted, because these systems were similar to those available on the audio market.

Situation 2: Free-Flowing Drinks

Diet beverages present another happy tale of innovative products with few corporate and customer barriers to hurdle.

With the growing health consciousness of U.S. customers, soft drinks without sugar and caffeine became a highly desired innovation. There were no usage pattern disruptions because the beverages were available at all the familiar outlets—supermarkets, restaurants, and vending machines—and in all the familiar packages. Nor was there any customer value barrier. In fact, most people felt that the diet beverages provided additional value when the caffeine and the calories were removed. Since the drinks did not have any significant image or perceived risk problems at the time, the market was wide open and waiting.

Beverage makers were ready to come marching in. Firms such as Pepsi, Coca-Cola, and RC Cola (which pioneered the product development) were not impeded by any structural corporate barriers in their charge into the diet market. Years of making soft drinks gave them access to all the ingredients as well as the production facilities to manufacture the diet variations. No special expertise was required to make the new products. Further, the diet drinks could be distributed to customers through the same channels long established for the regular soft drinks. Thus, diet beverages did not create operational barriers, resource barriers, or market access barriers for existing companies.

Diet soft drinks have been the fastest growing segment of the market. Today they constitute more than 30 percent of total soft drink consumption. As the population grows older, and people become more health and diet conscious—and as new sugar substitutes such as NutraSweet become available—diet soft drinks are likely to surpass regular versions in market share.

Situation 3: Banking for the Future

In 1982, the federal government offered Individual Retirement Accounts (IRAs) as a major tax incentive for the public to save. Each individual had a wide spectrum of investments to choose from: stocks, bonds, real estate income trusts, bank investments, and so on. Commercial banks realized the major opportunity they had to woo funds. They diversified their portfolio of products from just certificates of deposit to all possible investment vehicles. Further, they allowed customers the flexibility to switch their funds from one investment to another, as many times as they wanted. This switching could be done over the phone, if desired, and at no additional cost.

Banks faced no structural barriers in reorganizing themselves to compete in the IRA market. Customers had no problems in using banks for long-term savings; the IRAs were just a variation. They found it extremely convenient, in fact, to open IRAs with the same bank that had their checking/savings account. It saved customers the hassle of searching for an independent brokerage firm if they wished to invest, for example, in the stock market.

IRAs were an astonishing success. Not only were contributions to accounts deductible up to $2000 dollars, but interest income was tax deferred. They also appealed to people whose faith in the future had been shaken by several years of very high inflation and by the social security funding crisis. Billions of dollars were deposited, as a result, in commercial banks and savings and loan associations.

Situation 4: Math Made Easy

The digital watch story detailed earlier finds a ready parallel in the market development of electronic calculators. With both these innovations, firms with access to the digital and electronic technologies had no trouble manufacturing the products and making them available to the customer. The customers, in turn, offered no resistance to purchasing and using the calculators. The electronic variation was cheaper and required little learning—and their performance was well guaranteed. No usage disruption; no negative image associations; no risk.

STRATEGIC CONDITIONS

Experience Tells

For the G&G strategy to be effective, certain favorable conditions must be present. The first relates to experience.

> A firm must have access to experience curve benefits and must focus on overall cost-advantage if it wishes to be successful with the G&G strategy.

The story of electronic calculators and Texas Instruments (TI) aptly illustrates this requirement. Texas Instruments obtained a cost advantage in calculators by approaching from two fronts. First, they used offshore manufacturing operations to cut production costs. They built production plants in Spain, Mexico, Brazil, and Italy. The principal strategy was to increase capacity where the company already had semiconductor plants, thus minimizing startup and overhead costs. Second, the company achieved an increase in economies of scale from automated testing procedures and greater efficiencies in manufacturing, as the production volume increased. The company was thus able to decrease costs and pass the savings on to the customer. The increased cost efficiency was also an effective competitive weapon.

The success of TI's strategy was evident from the similar approaches adopted by their competitors. To cut costs, Bowmar began training assembly line personnel at a new plant in Nogales, Mexico, and Hewlett-Packard started an assembly facility in Penang, Malaysia. Further, several firms started pricing their products based on the same experience effect noted in the earlier discussion of digital watches.

In the beverage business, on the other hand, being the biggest was more important than being the first. 7-Up and RC Cola initiated the market for noncaffeine beverages, hammering away with an advertising theme that stressed history and health: "No caffeine. Never had it, never will. Don't you feel good about 7-Up?" Pepsi-Cola followed suit and also went after the sugar-free segment, hooking customers with its jingle: "Diet Pepsi, One small calorie, Now you see it, now you don't." Coca-Cola was at first an innocent bystander. However, once it became evident that a lucrative market existed for these products, Coca-Cola jumped right in. Coca-Cola could effectively compete in this segment, despite its late entry, because of the company's unique experience benefits. Coca-Cola, in fact, has been in the soft drink business longer than any other firm, and mass producing diet beverages was simple enough. So, it was not 7-Up and Pepsi alone that grabbed market share and grew. Coca-Cola reached a respectable position in the marketplace by capitalizing on experience.

But bigger is not necessarily better if you are carrying dead weight. When the long distance business was first deregulated, AT&T ran into difficulty. While they still had to subsidize the low local phone rates offered by their Bell Operating Companies (BOCs), the new entrants—MCI, Sprint, and Alnet—were able to attract customers with unencumbered lower prices for long distance calling. Based on their "50 percent cheaper than Bell" claim, for instance, MCI acquired more than a million accounts in three to four years.

The tide began to turn back, however, with final divestiture. Free of the BOCs and armed with a general mandate for equal access, AT&T could now compete as vigorously as MCI and the

Strategic Conditions

others. Once again, AT&T's dominant market share translates into significant cost advantages. Indeed, GTE-Sprint and Alnet have merged to become U.S. Sprint, and MCI is switching marketing focus to business customers in an attempt to counter AT&T's superior cost position.

All other common carriers have found that their network and marketing costs are too high to compete on price alone. Further, AT&T has been able to reduce rates as the access charges to BOCs are separated from long distance charges. The giant has thus been able to retain its customer base; nearly 90 percent of AT&T's profits come from long distance service.

The use of nylon—and, subsequently, plastics such as polyvinyl chloride—in packaging is an example of an industrial product that has attracted customers due to the lower costs. Plastics are being used in a wide variety of applications, such as packaging (foods, industrial goods, clothing) and automobile components (fenders). With increasing scope for applications, and therefore increasing production volume, the experience effect has become dominant in the manufacture of plastics. This, in turn, has allowed the larger producers to enjoy distinct cost advantages, which are passed on, at least partially, in the form of lower prices to customers.

Channels Open

For the G&G strategy to succeed, a firm must have a strong distribution system at its disposal.

Once again, the telecommunications industry provides a relevant case for consideration. Deregulation allowed innumerable competitors to enter the telephone equipment market in 1985. One of the few firms that succeeded, at least in the early days, was General Electric. GE already had an extensive distribution system of over 20,000 dealers that reached customers (including home building contractors) with products varying from toasters to major appliances such as ovens and refrigerators. Marketing its telephones through the powerful channel system was thus easy for GE and involved no additional cost.

As we saw earlier, Texas Instruments benefited from their experience advantage in calculator production. The company ultimately succeeded in the calculator market because they also had an excellent distribution network. TI made a conscious effort to help out their dealers. They provided price protection by wiring price changes a week in advance. TI also gave dealers credit on the difference between old and new prices for shipments made in the four-week period prior to a price change. The short notice period also prevented rumors from hurting sales and preserved the dealers' faith in TI. Highly satisfied dealers made it easy for the company to expand their retail network across the country. The distribution system grew even stronger, reducing TI's marketing costs. As a result, TI seized the chance to grab the electronic calculator market and grow.

Production experience and distribution also combined to help Japanese automakers when they attempted to enter the U.S. market in the mid 1960s. They already had a competitive advantage from lower production costs. The Japanese auto plants enjoyed the benefits of automation and a highly dedicated labor force that learned and improved very rapidly. The experience curve effect clearly gave them a cost advantage, but this alone would not have allowed the Japanese to penetrate the market. When they first arrived in the United States, the Japanese firms could not reach potential car buyers because they had no distribution system. Undaunted, they found the most effective solution. They convinced many dealers for General Motors (who then represented the largest network) and Ford that the small Japanese cars could be sold as a second car for the family, while the large U.S. cars could be the first car. The dealers were happy to find a complement to the domestic line because GM and Ford did not then make compact cars.

Once the Japanese cars had gained a foothold in the marketplace, their high performance–price (value) ratio won over the driving public. The rest of the success story is all too well known. Today, Japanese car makers such as Nissan (formerly Datsun), Toyota, and Honda dominate the U.S. market. The imports, primarily led by the Japanese, now constitute more than 25 percent of all automobile sales. In fact, the Japanese car makers (also Mitsubishi, Subaru, and Mazda) now outsell General Motors in the biggest car market, California.

Risky Business

For the Grab and Grow strategy to succeed, management must be willing to take high risks for long-term payoffs.

Once again, the Texas Instruments case is informative. Based on their calculations of lower costs of components, improved methods of assembly, and lower marketing costs in the foreseeable future, TI's management pursued a deliberate policy of price reductions on consumer calculators linked to volume production increases. By means of this price cutting, TI's management was taking a calculated risk that the company could hold on to their current market share until the sales volume increased. While most so-called scientific calculators were priced from $180 to $220, TI's SR-10 model was only $89.95, the SR-11 was $109.95, and the SR-20 was $139.95. The basic premise underlying TI's strategy was simple: If they could fend off competition for a while, their dealers, who were aware of the new low prices, could encourage customers to wait for delivery from Texas Instruments.

At the risk of never being able to recover its costs, TI achieved price leadership in the consumer calculator field at both ends of the pricing spectrum: The scientific calculators represented TI's high end, while they sold models to the general public for less than $10. The strategy succeeded because management was willing to play a risky game for the high returns over time.

A Better Mousetrap

For the G&G strategy to succeed, a firm must be capable of upgrading its products over the long run.

The original calculators performed only the basic arithmetic functions. Texas Instruments upgraded their calculators with technically sophisticated memory functions. They added capacity for finding square roots and percentages, and they added keys for lock-down memory, automatic overflow, and the fixed and floating decimal schemes. Portable calculators were also specially designed for statisticians, financial analysts, and engineers. Hand-held calculators and calculators with pen-light batteries and recharging units became available. Product improvement was occurring at a very rapid pace, and different segments of the market were being accessed just as rapidly. Thus, TI produced a continuous spate of new and improved calculators that allowed the company to grab an early lead in the market and grow.

The early success of Apple computers in the PC market is another example of a successful G&G strategy that was based on quick product upgrading. With the entry of IBM into the PC market, Apple had to do something fast. The Apple II, already on the market, was targeted for use in business, the home, and schools. Then came Macintosh, which offered the ability to access 32 pieces of information at a time, compared to 16 pieces for the IBM PC. Mac also allowed impressive graphic programs to be run and so appealed to universities and small- and medium-sized businesses. Finally, the new Lisa 2s were built to run the same operative system and programs used in the Macintosh. Apple pushed the innovation along by turning customers' old Lisas into new Lisa 2s for free. The Lisa was also positioned to appeal to university faculty members and senior management at medium-sized businesses. With the upgrading of its products—greater memory, user-friendly features such as the mouse, graphics capabilities—Apple was able to grab a foothold in the market and continue to grow.

CAVEATS

Before adopting the Grab and Grow strategy, you should heed the following warnings: (1) Do not *over*estimate the size of the market. (2) Make sure you have experience curve benefits that cannot be imitated. (3) Do not *under*estimate your competitors.

Ironically, Texas Instruments is a lesson in how Grab and Grow can go awry. For even as TI succeeded in the calculator market, they met with disaster in the PC market. To begin with, TI overestimated the size of the PC market. While most industrial analysts expected 1983 sales to be at least double those of 1982 sales (2.3 million units) and certainly no more than 5 million units, TI planned on total industry sales of 6.7 million units. TI expected an exceptional amount of growth in the market and expanded its manufacturing facilities to produce up to 50 percent of this grossly overestimated market size. As a result, there was an excess supply of PCs.

TI then initiated a price war, assuming that competitors would be unable to match their offering. TI gave a $100 discount on their popular 99/4A model, dropping the price to $199. Commodore International promptly retaliated, and the ensuing battle reached a stage where TI was forced to sell the PC at $99—about $15 to $20 below estimated manufacturing costs. The company could no longer enjoy the benefits of economies of scale. Other competitors were also caught in the price war and became its victims. Warner Communications, owner of Atari, was the first casualty, losing $18.9 million in the first quarter of 1983. Mattel, North American Phillips, and Activision followed. TI took a first-quarter loss of $50 million and a second quarter loss of $100 million.

While TI felt that a decrease in retail sales and industry price cutting were the chief causes for this setback, the fact remains that TI was caught in its own trap. The company assumed that the competition could not move down the experience curve as fast. On the hardware side, TI's cost declines had not kept pace with price drops as effectively as the competitors' had. For example, Commodore's VIC 20 sold for about $89 and had one-third fewer integrated circuit components than TI's.

TI also hoped that increased sales in software and auxiliary devices would compensate for losses in the PCs. But purchasers of a $100 PC were hardly willing to spend $400 on a disk drive. TI had neglected the psychology of high-end consumers—the buyers of a $300 product might have been more willing to buy expensive add-ons. Meanwhile, the price cutting had already begun for the software and auxiliary devices. Commodore cut the prices on most of their software by more than half, to around $20. TI's software was still priced at $30 to $40. Furthermore, while TI's software focused on education, their competitors produced software that could satisfy the hottest demand among customers—software that could be used to play video games.

TI's G&G strategy in the PC market thus failed because the company overlooked all three caveats: (1) TI overestimated the size of the market, thus leading to oversupply; (2) they did not have the unique benefits of the experience curve, which would have enabled them to endure a price war; and (3) they underestimated competitors, who not only achieved faster cost declines, but also met market needs more efficiently.

An easily imitated innovation is also fatal to the G&G strategy. When General Electric came out with the electric toothbrush in the early 1960s, competing firms flooded the market with 42 brands in just eight weeks, preventing easy market share acquisition. The growth in the production of telephone equipment of various shapes, sizes, and features since the deregulation of the telephone equipment market in 1980 is relevant also. Ignoring the potential power of the competition's response will prove

Caveats

disastrous when a firm seeks the G&G route for success with its innovation.

Finally, always be aware of the circumstances—detailed in this chapter—that suggest the selection of the Grab and Grow strategy over the other alternatives. One final illustration from G.D. Searle's introduction of Aspartame should drive the warning home.

Until 1982, the $12 billion-a-year U.S. market for sweeteners was controlled by sugar and two of its substitutes: saccharin and high-fructose corn syrup. Even though Americans loved sweet foods and drinks, they were becoming more and more conscious of the high calorie content of sugar. The per capita consumption of sugar declined from 102 pounds in 1972 to 89 pounds in 1981, and even further to 71 pounds in 1982. This decline in sugar consumption was matched by a growth in the market for high-fructose corn syrup. About 40 percent cheaper than sugar, high-fructose corn syrup was widely used by bakeries, soft drink bottlers, and producers of canned fruits and jams.

Meanwhile, artificial sweeteners became the most profitable segment of the market. Saccharin, about 300 times as sweet as sugar, had exclusive control of this segment. Besides its high sweetening properties, saccharin was also at least four times more economical than sugar. However, the Food and Drug Administration (FDA) tested the cancer-causing properties of saccharin and decided to ban it in 1977. A surge of protests from diabetics, weight watchers, and industry groups kept saccharin on the market until 1983.

Then Aspartame (more popularly known as NutraSweet) entered the market. Aspartame, produced by G.D. Searle, tasted as good as sugar and did not have the unpleasant, lingering aftertaste of saccharin. It had only a tiny fraction of sugar's calories and tasted 200 times sweeter. Just as important, it was able to obtain unqualified FDA approval for commercialization. The FDA considered Aspartame absolutely safe because it is a combination of two chemicals that occur in many common foods.

Furthermore, the body metabolizes Aspartame the same way as any other food.

With all these advantages, G.D. Searle ventured into the market. Under the trade name Equal, they launched an attack on the saccharin products being marketed for table-top use: Sweet 'N' Low, marketed by Cumberland Packing Corporation, and Sugar Twin, sold by Alberto-Culver. Simultaneously, under the brand name NutraSweet, Aspartame was sold as a sweetener for drink mixes, such as iced tea and Kool Aid, and for dry cereals. NutraSweet also entered the sweet puddings, gelatins, whipped toppings, and chewing gum markets. Lipton added a new tea mix to its product line—tea mix sweetened with Aspartame—priced identical to the tea mix sweetened with sugar. General Foods, which commands a significant share of the packaged powdered drink market, introduced Aspartame-sweetened counterparts for their Kool Aid and Country Time Lemonade. Aspartame, when used in these drinks, has an additional benefit: It does not cause tooth decay. Quaker Oats also introduced Aspartame into a new cereal called Halfsies; the dry cereal used only half as much sugar as other sweetened cereals, and Aspartame supplied the other half.

The approval for Aspartame's use in diet sodas having been granted in early 1984, G.D. Searle won yet another prize market. Canadian markets for diet drinks already carried Aspartame, and manufacturers discovered that drinks containing the artificial sweetener maintained their sweetness for six to nine months—longer than the shelf life of most beverages.

G.D. Searle, however, priced its product at nearly twice that of sugar (and several times more than saccharin). The logic behind the pricing strategy was similar to that followed by most companies: The patent for Aspartame would expire in 1987, and Searle wanted to recover its R&D costs and the costs of waiting for FDA patent approval. Searle's product gained some acceptance in the market despite the high price, reflecting the company's belief that the additional benefits of Aspartame would outweigh the cost disadvantage.

Thus, Searle developed the market using the Slow and Steady strategy. However—and here is the key point—Searle could achieve an even higher share of the market and even better market entrenchment if they would switch to a Grab and Grow strategy. The economies of scale available from the large production volume, coupled with the advantage of being the sole manufacturer, would protect the company against future competitive threats. A patented new artificial sweetener could enter the market after 1987 and pose problems for Aspartame, even before it achieved a significant share of the market, should Searle continue the current S&S strategy.

For the end user (the general public), artificial sweeteners in place of sugar do not drastically alter the mode of consumption of soft drinks, cereals, desserts, and other goods. Hence, Aspartame should be viewed as a continuous innovation to the packaged food customer. Since G.D. Searle has gained significant expertise in manufacturing Aspartame, the innovation is continuous to the supplier as well. With the threat of competitive entry soon after patent expiration, a G&G strategy is likely to be more effective at this stage of market development. G.D. Searle should try to Grab and Grow now while the corporate and consumer barriers are low and easily overcome.

SUMMARY

The Grab and Grow strategy works well when the firm is structurally ready to produce the innovation and the market is ready to use it. G&G is a mass market strategy that capitalizes on early entry. Experience yields greater cost efficiency, which can be translated into rapid growth and a strong competitive position. Initially, prices are below production costs as a customer base is built. Short-term sacrifices result, however, in long-term payoffs in market share and profitability.

High quality factory-installed car stereos, diet drinks, IRAs, and electronic calculators all had the qualifications for Grab and

Grow, and all took advantage of low customer and corporate barriers to find success in the marketplace.

A firm using the G&G strategy must have access to experience curve benefits and concentrate on creating an overall cost advantage. A strong distribution system is also a necessity. Further, companies must be willing to take risks for long-term payoffs and be able to upgrade their products over the long haul. Management cannot afford to overestimate the size of the market or underestimate the ability of the competition.

Not all innovations face combined low barriers—and not all innovating firms in that position recognize and exploit their opportunities. We next examine cases in which conditions are mixed: where customer resistance is high and corporate structural problems are low.

Bernstein, P.W. "Seven-Up's Sudden Taste for Cola." *Fortune*, May 17, 1982, 101–103.

Lyons, J., et al. "Electronics Statistical and Marketing Report: Calculators/Digital Watches." *Merchandising Week*, July 28, 1975, 36–43.

McElroy, J. "High Tech Dashboards." *Automotive Industries*, Aug, 1982, 21–24.

"Digital Watches: Bringing Watchmaking Back to the U.S." *Business Week*, Oct. 27, 1975, 78–81.

"Calculator Shakeout Forecast." *Electronic News*, Nov. 30, 1970, 20.

"Patterns in Pricing: Calculated Decline." *Electronic News*, June 4, 1973, 22.

"Patterns in Pricing: TI's Calculated Risk." *Electronic News*, Feb. 18, 1974, 27.

Forbes, Nov. 7, 1983, 256.

"Comparison of Electronic and Electromechanical Calculators. " *Office*, Sept. 1968, 161–164.

"Sales Boom, Prices Plummet in Pocket Calculators." *Purchasing*, Nov. 19, 1974, 65–67.

"New Chrysler II Car to Have Stereo Radio." *Automotive News*, Feb. 6, 1984, 6.

"Seven Up Uncaps a Cola and an Industry Fued." *Business Week*, March 22, 1982, 97–98.

7
The Pick and Protect Strategy

As often as not, an innovative product or service will not face either of the extreme situations (that is, all high or all low barriers) that we have discussed in the previous two chapters. Firms looking to market their innovations may instead encounter a combination of high corporate and low customer barriers, or the reverse case of few structural corporate problems coupled with strong customer resistance. We will investigate the first variation in chapter 8. In this chapter, our center of interest is with the innovation going up against tough customer hurdles. In such an instance, firms should select the Pick and Protect (P&P) strategy, as illustrated in Figure 7.1.

Since customer barriers are high, the firm has to pick the *right application* for which the innovation creates the highest value for the customer. The customer should be willing to use the new product because of the singularly unique benefit it provides.

Once a firm develops a strong customer base for the product, its primary objective must be to protect itself from competitors

184   **The Pick and Protect Strategy**

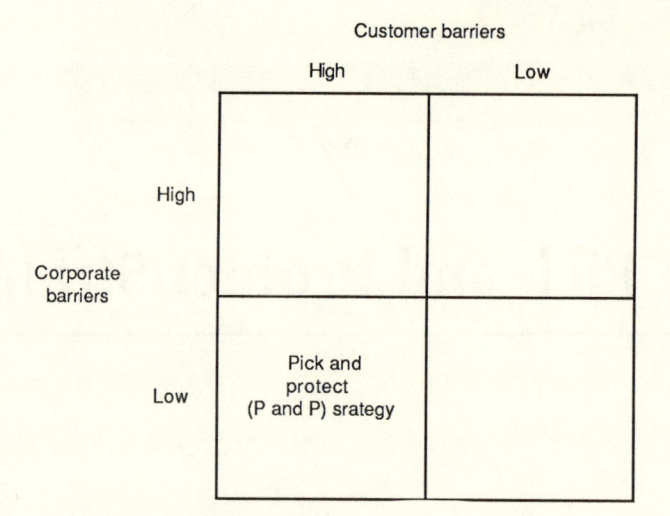

```
                    Customer barriers
                   High              Low
                 ┌─────────────┬─────────────┐
                 │             │             │
            High │             │             │
                 │             │             │
  Corporate      │             │             │
  barriers       ├─────────────┼─────────────┤
                 │   Pick and  │             │
            Low  │   protect   │             │
                 │ (P and P)   │             │
                 │  srategy    │             │
                 └─────────────┴─────────────┘
```

Figure 7.1. Strategy matrix: Pick and Protect

who are lured by the chance of profits. Since the corporate barriers for the innovation are low, competitive entry is a distinct possibility. The P&P strategy is thus ideal when the firm is quite ready to market the innovation, but the customer faces high discontinuity in using it.

STRATEGIC OCCASIONS

The Pick and Protect strategy can be used successfully when innovations face low corporate and high customer barriers.

Once again, these conditions can be found across a wide range of economic activities. As in previous chapters, we will first detail several representative situations before examining the P&P strategic variations.

Situation 1: Warming up in the Right Niche

Our first illustration is in the sometimes delicate field of medical services: the use of thermography to detect breast cancer and other physical abnormalities.

Thermography is essentially a physical (pictorial or sound) representation of the variations in temperature over a given surface. The properties of thermography have been known since the early nineteenth century. The technology has been freely available to any firm that sought its application. The corporate barriers to the access and use of the innovation have been low.

First of all, detecting and capturing the temperature differences in the human body is a known expertise. Therefore, when a Canadian pathologist conclusively demonstrated that a cancer cell is invariably hotter than a normal cell by at least one degree Fahrenheit, the issue became simply how to design an affordable product for the doctors and the patients. With the advent of electronics, it was also easy to manufacture an electronic box with a probe on standard assembly line principles using off-the-shelf technology and parts.

Thus, there were no resource constraints, since product development and manufacturing on existing facilities can be accomplished for under $250,000. Nor were there any regulatory issues, at least in the early days of thermography-based medical electronics. While the Food and Drug Administration had very stringent testing and certification procedures for drugs, it had established no comparable guidelines for medical electronics. Indeed, all you needed was an Underwriters Laboratory (UL) seal for product safety. Finally, there was no barrier to market access because medical electronics could be sold to hospitals, doctors, and even directly to the public. The only market access barrier had to do with the clinical evaluation of the technology to demonstrate that thermography performed as well as or better than the most popular existing mammography technology.

On the other hand, there were significant market barriers. The primary customers were physicians, who were not trained on the use of thermography for cancer detection. There were also significant perceived risk factors. For example, the doctors were concerned about the reliability of the new technology. They did not want to switch from the traditional mammography partly because of the fear of legal suits for malpractice or negligence. Also, they did not know whether the product had any side effects. (It did not.)

There was also considerable hesitation among doctors, clinics, and hospitals because of tradition and image barriers. Most of them were unwilling to experiment with the new technology because of the fear that they might be labeled as radical and inclined to experiment with human life. Most medical facilities were content to let the university hospitals and leading-edge research clinics do the preliminary testing and evaluation.

Situation 2: Fair Game on any Turf

Chemistrand, the textile division of Monsanto, developed a synthetic grass surface called chemgrass, the earliest form of the artificial turf that we have today. Monsanto had no problems in coming out with the innovation: They had the financial resources, technical expertise, and operational facilities available. However, artificial turf was resisted by the potential end users—the athletes who had to play on it.

Professional baseball and football players felt (and many still feel) that synthetic surfaces would take a few years off their careers. Because a hard, uniform surface allows people to run faster and change direction more quickly, it puts a greater strain on muscles and connective tissue and generates more forceful contact between athletes as well as between athletes and the playing field itself. Furthermore, the artificial surface retains rather than absorbs heat; it also generates higher temperatures through greater friction. The heat is transferred directly to the body through the shoes. The result is uncomfortable feet, heat stress, and exhaustion. All of this added up to considerable uncertainty for the athletes destined to play on the surface and for the team and stadium owners—the actual purchasers of the new substance—who employed (and invested in) them.

Situation 3: Sweet-Smelling Macho Man

With the exception of lightly perfumed after-shave lotions and the all-purpose traditional bay rum, cosmetics for men were generally frowned upon in the early 1900s. Many men went so far as to forbid barbers to sprinkle scented tonic on them. Traditionally, cosmetics had always been associated with women. How could a man stoop to using something so effeminate and violate such an entrenched cultural taboo?

The concept of male cosmetics was thus severely resisted by men until the 1960s. For the manufacturers, however, making cosmetics for men was not a problem, especially if they were already manufacturing such products for women. Production facilities and technical know-how was the same, too, and the raw materials (chemicals) were already on hand. The firms thus faced no corporate barriers whatsoever in switching from the ladies' market to the men's. But there were significant customer barriers.

Situation 4: Beware the Soft in Software

Computer software development faces very few corporate barriers. First, the expertise to write software is almost global today. In fact, countries like India and China are becoming major suppliers of complex software packages because the know-how is spreading. Second, creating a software package or product requires no major changes in the current operations of a company because new software development is always a separate project that requires only the use of a computer on a shared basis. Third, software development is usually not as expensive as hardware, depending on the complexity. Most applications programs can be put together in less than six months and be fully tested in the field in less than one year. Fourth, there are also very few regulatory barriers, except perhaps infringement of other people's copyrights. Even here, the regulation is relatively weak and ambiguous, since most software development is considered in the public domain, similar to a computer language. Finally, market access is not a serious barrier, because the large computer companies such as IBM, DEC, Hewlett-Packard, and Burroughs (now merged with Sperry) actually encourage independent companies or individuals to create software.

On the other hand, software users face several market barriers. First of all, software packages are not compatible with all computer systems. They are usually designed to work on specific types of computers (mainframe, minicomputers, or microcomputers) as well as on specific operating systems (Assembler, Unix, MS/DOS, etc.). If the user does not have the comparable hardware and operating system, he or she is unable to incorporate the new software package. Second, each software program is unique. The purchaser must then learn how to effectively use the software. He or she needs considerable education, training, and practice to feel comfortable with the new software. Third, it is often not clear whether the new software is better than existing programs, especially in the area of mainframes and minicomputers. Further, while there are no real image problems, a new software product often suffers from a perception of risk on the part of the users. They often worry that the new software may destroy their database and create errors. They are concerned that there are bugs to be removed and even that they may have made a total mistake in selecting the package.

Situation 5: The Diesel Car Nearly Loses Steam

Motivated by the energy crisis of the 1970s, automobile manufacturers such as General Motors and Volkswagen proceeded to replace gasoline engines with diesel engines in some of their models to meet government fuel efficiency requirements for their cars. The incorporation of the diesel engine into the design did not have any adverse effect on the auto production or assembly process. Nor did it impose financial or technical hardships on the auto firms. Thus, the innovation did not generate any resistance from the suppliers' side.

The customers, however, experienced several barriers (as we noted in chapter 2). First, diesel was available at few gas stations. Some of these gas stations were interested only in large-volume sales to truck drivers and frowned on the hapless auto owners. Thus, the very availability of diesel fuel was the first problem customers had to face. Second, maintenance of the diesel engine was quite different from that of the gasoline engine; customers had to be trained to take care of the car properly. Early diesel engines were really converted gasoline engines and experienced significant breakdowns after 50,000 miles. This produced a barrage of customer complaints. Finally, several customers found that the diesel engines were smelly and sometimes very difficult to start. Thus, diesel engine automobiles faced severe customer resistance despite corporate eagerness to produce them.

STRATEGIC VARIATIONS

At first glance, all of these situations seem almost hopeless. Each generates considerable customer resistance, either because of uncertainties or inconveniences. Judiciously applied, however, the Pick and Protect strategy can overcome these obstacles and achieve a measure of success for the innovations in the marketplace. As before, a few conditions must be met.

> The innovation has to be customized so that it comes as close as possible to satisfying the need of a particular market segment.

Thermography: The Need to Know

Thermography became successful as a commercialized technology because it was customized for the detection of breast cancer. The odds of an American woman getting breast cancer are one in eleven today. The disease often brings physical disfigurement and psychological trauma, and the mortality rate is very high. For example, more than 37,000 U.S. women died of breast cancer in 1982. The increasing number of working women and their subsequent postponement of pregnancy has increased this risk even more. The major problem with the disease is that it can go undetected for a long time. A tumor one centimeter in diameter, the smallest that can be identified by a doctor through palpation, represents eight years of cancerous growth. By the time a woman realizes that she has a lump in her breast, the tumor is 3.5 centimeters in diameter, and her chances of survival have dropped to 38 percent. While there is no cure for breast cancer, scientists and physicians agree that early detection of a tumor greatly increases the survival rate. Mammography, an X-ray technique, can be used to detect the presence of breast lumps, but X rays are radiation hazards that should be avoided by women with a history of breast cancer in their families.

Thermography offered a solution, using its end products: thermograms. Similar in appearance to weather maps, thermograms are full-color thermal patterns of the heat radiating from the skin. For example, the lowest temperature is displayed as dark brown; it changes with progressive temperature elevation to yellow, green, and blue. The technology is capable of identifying cancers because they give off more heat than normal tissue.

Vectra International Corporation, a small research firm in Columbia, Maryland, developed a method to correlate the different shades of a thermogram to information about breast cancer. This method was known as the Cholestric Analysis Profile (CAP) and was based on liquid crystal technology. The CAP uses liquid crystals encapsulated in flat plates to provide an accurate estimate of breast temperatures. Based on temperature differences, each of the six thin plates changes colors, and the process is recorded using a camera with high-speed polaroid film. The CAP thus detects cancerous lumps by color. The success of the specific application of thermography to detection of a particularly dreaded disease broke down customer resistance. Thermography could be sold to doctors—and hence to patients—as a reliable, early-diagnosis device for breast cancer. It was this niche that Vectra International astutely picked for itself and proceeded to protect.

Software Firms Up

In the early 1960s, software was required mostly for the big, expensive mainframe computers. But with the proliferation of smaller systems, software manufacturers had to deal with data processing managers who refused to accept standardized software. Sales representatives had to call on these managers at regular intervals and develop specialized packages written in FORTRAN and COBOL, the popular languages. Thus, most software firms had to pick one of three niches in which to operate:

1. Applications software designed for tasks such as accounting and payroll. *Wordstar* of MicroPro, *Multiplan* of Microsoft, and *Visicalc* of Visicorp are examples.
2. Utility software, which mainly helped computer programmers write programs (e.g., *dBaseII* of Ashton-Tate).
3. Systems control software, which handles basic housekeeping operations such as controlling the printer and memory (e.g., *MS/DOS*, from Microsoft).

Within each niche, a firm had to specialize in specific software packages to remain competitive. For example, Via Computer developed the *Microprophit* package, the personal computer version of powerful corporate planning software that had run on mainframe computers for 15 years. *Microprophit* could handle 9000-line models, whereas most spreadsheets could handle only 255-line models.

Another way that software firms protect themselves is by picking the right computer and developing a successful package for it. The rationale is that choosing a computer that is least resisted by customers is one way of gaining acceptance for the software as well. Choosing the right computer model, however, can be a high-risk proposition, and picking the industry giants does not guarantee safety, either. For instance, Sierra On-Line and several other software companies invested considerable resources in developing software for the IBM PCjr. However, the sale of the PCjr remained flat for a long time, thus adversely affecting the software sales as well.

The truth, though, is that there are no generalizations. While several software companies failed to make it under the IBM banner, Software Publishing Corporation succeeded. They went after the segment of first-time users who needed easy-to-operate software. They tailor-made software for these customers and priced their product way below competitive offerings ($150 compared to the competitors' average of $300). Once the success of the software became evident, IBM took the entire line of software under its own label.

Some software manufacturers have been forced to stick with successful computer makers, even if the latter are uncooperative. For example, Commodore gives technical help to only those software companies that allow Commodore to market their programs. These software companies sometimes have to content themselves with a royalty of only 5 percent, as opposed to the industry norm of 20 percent. But the need for survival forces these firms to play along. Niching, then, may not lead to unlimited riches, but it does provide a customer base that can be nurtured.

For the Athlete's Foot

With all the potential problems that athletes perceived in the use of artificial turf, Monsanto had to find an application for which the innovation would be an excellent solution. Their search led them to the realm of urban education.

City schools had several problems in designing playgrounds. First of all, there was tremendous pressure from parents to have good facilities built for their children. Several educators themselves advocated the construction of these facilities when they discovered that city children were less physically fit than those from small towns. One reason for this disparity was that children from smaller towns played on grass-covered playgrounds, whereas the asphalt surfaces of city playgrounds inhibited children from running and playing at full speed due to the risk of injury. Further, city schools always had to cope with the problem of lack of space. Even if they wished to build a playground, they did not own sufficient land on which to do so.

It was for these city schools that the synthetic turf developed by Monsanto proved to be a boon. First, the turf playground could be used to furnish playing areas for nongrass sports such as tennis or volleyball. Second, it was softer to the skin than asphalt, and thus the risk of serious injury was minimized. Parents and school authorities were considerably pleased with this property of the new product. Finally, the synthetic turf was inexpensive to maintain. This economic factor proved to be the clincher. Monsanto thus picked a good market niche for its innovation: the schools in big cities that required a safe and viable substitute for the asphalt playgrounds they did have and the grass playgrounds they could never get.

It's Okay to Smell Nice

Manufacturers of cosmetics for the male market have, over the years, employed a series of repositioning strategies and have achieved remarkable success. Initially, the advent of the safety razor opened up the market for lathers and lotions. These were sold by stressing functional and medical qualities, such as skin protection and conservation of facial moisture. Scent or fragrance was not mentioned at all.

Next came deodorants. These were to be used by men, not necessarily to make them smell good, but to prevent them from smelling bad. It was, however, not until the early 1960s that the traditional obstacles were partially overcome, and fragrance per se became a selling point of male after-shaves and colognes. Even then, strictly masculine appeals were used: The scents in the product were he-man, woodsy, or distinguished. All these appeals were designed to create an aura of increasing maleness, as demonstrated by a number of specific appeals: sexy (English Leather), athletic (Brut), high status (Aramis), macho (Jaguar), and even fashionable (Cardin).

Clearly, male resistance to the idea of using cosmetics was slowly overcome as cosmetic manufacturers developed market niches and adopted appropriate promotional messages directed to validating each niche.

The Diesel Begins to Move

In order to overcome market resistance in the late 1970s and early 1980s, auto manufacturers positioned diesel cars as fuel economy vehicles offering high gas mileage. Also, the price of diesel fuel was well below that of regular gasoline, and this enhanced the fuel efficiency (in terms of miles per dollar) even further. The distribution network for diesel fuel rapidly expanded across the country until there were about 20,000 service stations (almost one in every seven) that could service the cars. This *minimum* availability, plus the ecological appeal of low emissions, plus fuel economy allowed auto makers to develop a market niche for diesel engine cars. As we saw in chapter 2, diesel cars never had any real prospect of generating mass market appeal.

Strategic Variations

Unfortunately, even this short happy story did not continue ever after. As the price of gasoline crashed in 1986, the popularity of diesel engines subsided. Also, car makers were using diesel engines as a transition strategy until they could improve fuel efficiency of the regular gasoline engine. In the early 1980s, GM, Ford, and Chrysler produced highly fuel-efficient gasoline engines that began to compete with diesel. Thus, when gasoline became cheaper than diesel fuel, the regular gasoline engine became a better value.

> A firm must be aggressive once it picks a niche, or else competitors may decide to grab a piece of the action.

Establishing and retaining market presence is very critical to firms using the P&P strategy. As the following cases illustrate, a niche once won must be defended.

In the software industry, for instance, firms had to win and retain space on already crowded retail shelves. Directory listings suggest that there are at least 11,000 software firms creating about 20,000 to 40,000 programs. Yet no supplier has even a 10 percent share of the market; only six firms have more than 1 percent of the market: Visicorp, Microsoft, MicroPro, Digital Research, Ashton-Tate, and Peachtree (MSA). Except for these bigger firms, software companies have had to survive by developing specific application programs for customers and then customizing them even more.

Once Vectra International Corporation had developed the market for thermography in the detection of breast cancer, the company set about strengthening that position. They made themselves more acceptable to physicians by setting up a laboratory to receive and analyze plate photographs. Vectra's staff of trained technicians were thus able to see thousands of plates in a year. Research was conducted in France, because European physicians were more receptive to thermography. Based on the analysis of the Vectra plates by the French National Institution of Health and Medical Research, the company set up a classification system for cancer victims. This system served as a central reference base for physicians throughout the world and hastened the acceptance of the technology everywhere, including the United States. Vectra thus fortified their position in the segment that they had chosen to serve: doctors and clinics that diagnose and treat cancer patients.

CAVEATS

If your firm is in a position to use the Pick and Protect strategy to market an innovation, you should be aware of two important dangers. First, unless you have the advantage of being the early entrant in a market segment, you may have already lost out to those firms that made the first move.

In all the examples that we have considered in this chapter, it is evident that the early entrant enjoyed the greatest advantage in terms of market penetration. In the case of diesel engines, General Motors and Volkswagen were the beneficiaries. In software development, giants like VisiCorp and Ashton-Tate capitalized on early entry. Vectra International was the winner in the thermography market by virtue of entering early in the game. Monsanto reaped the benefits of early development in marketing synthetic turf.

Second, you must never underestimate the competition's ability to attack and move into your niche. Complacency is dangerous because success in a given segment may be short lived. Hence, your firm needs to be on the lookout for newer segments into which it can move and establish itself.

This truth is probably more dramatically illustrated in the personal computer field than any other industry. Only a year ago, it seemed that IBM was a runaway dominant supplier of PCs, and everyone was developing IBM compatible software. Today, IBM's market share has been declining dramatically at the same time that many IBM compatibles are gaining. The same phenomenon is occurring in the software business. Who would have imagined that Microsoft would emerge as a major software company in less than five years? The early leaders, including Ashton-Tate and Lotus, were perceived to be unstoppable. Finally, remember such computer companies as Atari, Intellivision, and even Texas Instruments? They all left the computer business in less than 10 years.

The primary reasons are simple. All of these businesses have very low corporate barriers. Therefore it is very easy for competition to enter the field, improve on the performance–price ratio, and take the market away—unless the innovator establishes a strong niche position and defends it vigorously.

SUMMARY

The Pick and Protect strategy applies when corporate barriers are low and customer barriers are high. Firms must choose the right application; that is, the one that creates the greatest value for the customer. Once that customer base is established, it must be defended against competition lured in by low corporate barriers.

Pick and Protect has been the correct choice for a number of innovative products and services. Thermography to detect breast cancer, artificial surfaces for school playgrounds, beauty aids for men, and software specialized for particular business needs are examples. The diesel engine did reasonably well with the P&P strategy before environmental changes put the brakes on.

In P&P, the innovation should be customized to satisfy the unique needs of a particular market segment. Once selected, the market niche must be fought for aggressively. It is vital, therefore, to be the first entrant into the chosen battleground. Complacency is very dangerous. Even IBM has had to struggle to maintain PC market position against new competitors.

In the next chapter we will examine conditions under which the last of our four strategies, the Migrate and Maintain strategy, is appropriate.

Bassin, A. "The Kiss of Life." *Drugs: Cosmetics Industry*, Oct. 1980, 321.

———. "The Cloning of the Male." *Drugs: cosmetics Industry*, March 1981, 201.

———. "The Macho Mystique," *Drugs: Cosmetics Industry*, May 1982, 301.

Donath, B., "Can Your New Product Pass this Test?: How to Score Its Chances with the Sheth New Product Screen." *Business Marketing*, July 1984, 66–68.

Maxwell, N. "Old Taboos Have Faded Away." *Drugs: Cosmetics Industry*, May 1975, 42–44.

Maher, P. "Software Marketing Madness." *Business Marketing*, March 1984, 78.

Meyers, J., & Fournier, J. "Thermography: A Medical Surveillance Tool?" *National Safety News*, May 1983, 37–38.

Milap, C.R. "Consumer Tech the Key to Software Marketing." *Business Marketing*, March 1984, 86.

Norris, E. "Thermography Maps Injuries." *Business Insurance*, Feb. 23, 1981, 1.

Smith, M. "Software Services." *Forbes*, March 28, 1983, 61–76.

"Market Develops for Software Distribution Specialists." *Electronic News*, July 12, 1982, 18.

"Beating Breast Cancer—The CAP Test." *Forbes*, Dec. 6, 1982, 196.

8
The Migrate and Maintain Strategy

The flip side of the combination of smooth corporate structures and strong customer resistance also presents a unique set of difficulties. When your innovation faces only token customer constraints but significant corporate barriers, your firm should select the Migrate and Maintain (M&M) strategy (see Figure 8.1).

In this strategy, you maintain your customer base by migrating them to an improved version of your product or service. Since your customers are already happy with the original offering and satisfied with its value, they should be even more pleased to have an even better variation available. Thus, the M&M approach allows you to protect your market from competitive threats. By constantly being one up in terms of product development, you can keep competitors at bay and preserve customer loyalty.

	Customer barriers	
	High	Low
High		"Migrate and maintain" (M and M) strategy
Low		

(Corporate barriers on vertical axis)

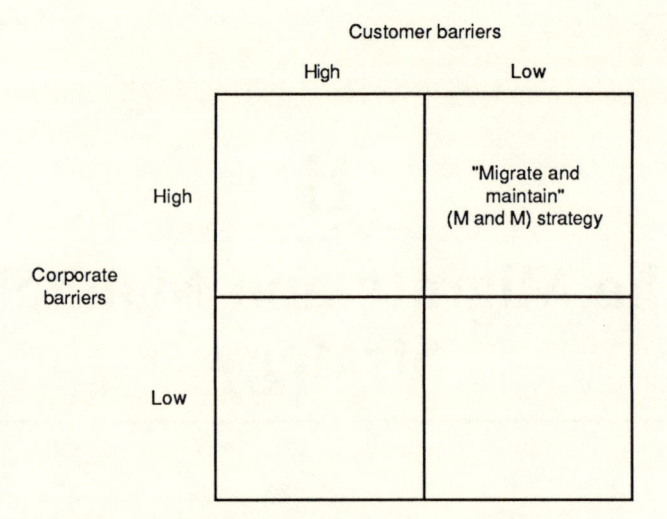

Figure 8.1. Strategy matrix: Migrate and Maintain

STRATEGIC OCCASIONS

Once again, the scope of the M&M strategy is practically economy-wide. Consider the following representative situations.

Situation 1: The Jumbo Jets Take Off

Boeing's 747 jumbo jet was developed in the 1970s and was hailed as one of the major technological breakthroughs of the decade. The jumbo was part of Boeing's ongoing and relentless efforts to upgrade aircraft and so maintain the loyalty of their customers. Even though product enhancement is central to the company's culture, advances such as the jumbo jet create structural problems.

First, the aerodynamics of such a big aircraft required a nontraditional design, especially in terms of lift, electronics, and fuel utilization. Second, jumbo jets generated massive changes in operations because the size of the aircraft was not compatible with the Boeing 707 that it replaced. Boeing needed to find new suppliers for parts, to make new assembly arrangements, and to develop new electronics. Third, the company had to make a multibillion dollar investment in the 1960s, which was not recovered until the 1980s. There were significant regulatory barriers as well. The new generation of wide-body aircraft had to be certified by the FAA, a long process.

In contrast, customer impediments to innovative results were low. The airlines were happy to migrate to the new models of the Boeing fleet because they received ever-increasing price–performance ratios with each shift upward. In the late 1970s, for instance, Boeing aircraft had the lowest seat-mile operating cost: 1.75 cents.

Situation 2: Big Blue Becomes Bigger

A long, long time ago (in 1960), there was only the IBM 1400 series of computers. And the majority of the market was satisfied. International Business Machines was not. IBM came up with the revolutionary 360 series, which could perform higher order calculations at a faster rate and a much lower cost. The 360 series was announced in 1964 by IBM. Within the next three years, IBM had overcome the teething problems with hardware and software. By 1967, 50 percent of IBM's customers had migrated to the 360 series. By 1969, this figure had increased to 70 percent.

Once a large customer base was established for the IBM 360 series, firms began to offer hardware that could be plugged into IBM systems as replacements for IBM peripheral equipment. These competitors came to be known as Plug-Compatible Manufacturers (PCMs), and they manufactured tape drives, disk drives, and high-speed line printers. By offering lower priced products and superior technology, the PCMs began to erode

IBM's market for peripherals. Even the PCM's sales forces were made up of ex-IBM personnel.

IBM finally realized the threat and retaliated. They introduced the 370 series, which would migrate customers to a superior product and expose only the few who remained with the 360 series to competition. The 370 was designed as an all integrated semiconductor hardware computer with advanced software and lower production costs than the 360 series.

IBM planned two other major improvements in the operating systems of the 370 series. First, the new system processed several programs simultaneously (i.e., multiprogramming). Second, a new feature called virtual memory allowed allocation of core memory to programs whenever necessary, rather than in fixed increments. Both features were based on a combination of hardware capability and specially designed software. IBM estimated that the 370 series would offer at least a twofold improvement over the 360 series. But the expected impact of the IBM 370 was nullified by competition from other systems manufacturers, who beat IBM to the draw and introduced similar systems even before IBM's announcement.

In August 1971, IBM began deliveries of the 370 series. The PCMs, however, quickly entered the market with peripherals. Even though IBM tried to buy time by introducing technical changes in the peripherals and by cutting prices, the PCMs quickly overcame the technological changes and matched the price drops. IBM needed something far more effective to shake off the PCMs and retain their customer base. The need became more critical as customers continued to invest in peripherals; by 1975, 70 percent of the hardware dollar was being spent on these accessories.

At this point, IBM created yet another turning point in the industry by announcing the 4300 series. The 4300 system offered a sevenfold increase in price–performance ratio. Further, the system could be used anywhere—not just in an air-conditioned environment—and it was compatible with other systems. With all these advantages, IBM once again seized the initiative: all their customers migrated to the 4300 series. In migrating customers to the newer versions of its product, IBM had to overcome several corporate barriers: operational, financial, and expertise. IBM's customers, however, were quite content to adopt the innovative computer because it did not disrupt usage patterns.

Situation 3: Phones Became Upward, Mobile, and Cellular

Cellular radio telephones are the latest in communications technology. The basic principle in cellular phones is dividing a radio telephone service area into small territories called cells, each with its own low-power radio stations connected to the telephone switching system. Dividing the service area this way helps reduce busy signals by permitting repeated use of the same radio frequencies. It is thus much easier to get an open line from a car than it was with the previous mobile telephone service. Earlier, only a dozen customers could use the systems at the same time, since each metropolitan area had been assigned only 12 channels, all of which were broadcast from a single antenna. The users of this service had to wait as much as 30 minutes for a dial tone.

In contrast, cellular systems permit simultaneous conversations. As a car moves from cell to cell, the conversation is automatically handed by a computer from one antenna to the next. With a minimum of 48 channels per cell available, the cellular system can handle up to 50,000 calls per hour; the earlier mobile phone could handle only 1400. The quality of sound reception in a cellular system is as good as that from a desk phone in the home or office since the car is never far from a transmitter.

The manufacture of cellular phones is, however, quite different from the standard models. Each phone unit has a power source (a 3-pound box mounted in the car trunk), an antenna, a cable, and the phone itself, which rests in a cradle on the floor or on the dashboard. The system has to be designed for safety against unauthorized use or theft. Users are assigned a code number. If stolen, the system's computer can stop calls to and from the unit. The system also has a built-in memory for up to 10 telephone numbers, which can be dialed by simply pressing a button. There is also an on/off switch that permits cutting off incoming calls if necessary; callers will hear a recorded message explaining that the owner is not in the car.

Thus, while manufacturers of cellular phones have to put up with a totally new technology, customers enjoy the benefits of a new product with minimum effort. Nothing has changed in terms of operating the telephone system. On the contrary, it is more handy and offers more features than the desktop phone. Despite the high internal barriers for the manufacturer, the low customer barriers have allowed accelerated market development (see chapter 4 for a barrier-by-barrier analysis).

Situation 4: Computerized Triptiks

In 1984, Chrysler unveiled their latest electronic gadget in a sports car at the New Orleans World's Fair. The system used radio signals from satellites to pinpoint the vehicle's location on a computerized map. The glove compartment had been replaced with a video display screen.

At the beginning of a trip, the U.S. map (stored on a laser videodisc) appeared on the screen. By touching the screen, the driver could zoom in on any section of the map and could even get a detailed map of a state or a city. The computerized system could also continuously monitor the exact location of the car, which showed up as a symbol on the screen and moved across the map as the car traveled on a highway. The computer could also display the best route to a location.

Ford and GM have similar systems, except they currently use videotape cartridges to store the map data. All three automo-

Strategic Occasions

bile manufacturers have taken advantage of moves by major map makers, such as the American Automobile Association (AAA), to encode their maps in digital computer data, so that information such as recent road construction can be updated.

These automobile locaters depend on a military satellite navigation system called Navstar. The federal government expects to have launched 18 navigation satellites into space by 1988. These satellites will blanket the globe with radio signals and allow computers to calculate the location of an object within a few feet.

However, opinion in the Pentagon is divided as to whether access should be provided to these satellites for commercial use, because the same satellites would be used by the Defense Department. Commercial entrepreneurs, such as the Geostar Corporation of Princeton, New Jersey, also hope to build a low-cost navigation system that will be more sophisticated than Navstar. Geostar believes its system could be more cost-effective than Navstar because it would use a network of central computers rather than have computers in each automobile. The computers would serve as radio-receiver transmitters and would display data on small screens.

In any case, automobile makers will run into several structural problems. First, they must install this navigation system in the dashboard, where there is very limited space. They must also integrate the system with other microprocessors already in the car to monitor speed, distance, and fuel consumption. The navigation system has to be built to a level of reliability where lawsuits for product failure are unlikely. In addition, the automakers must obtain Department of Transportation approval for product safety. Finally, the system requires massive amounts of up-front expenditure, with the hope that consumers will readily buy the new technology.

For the customer, on the other hand, the new technology has generated few problems. For instance, computers are already performing jobs in cars: controlling engine functions, monitoring brakes, or tracking gas mileage. One model of the 1985 Buick

Riviera contains a cathode-ray-tube video screen that displays a wide range of technical information for the driver.

All this represents disruptive technology to the manufacturers, but imposes hardly any change on the customers. To people who love luxury cars, a video map is just another luxury. Car owners do not need to know how the satellites relay the information to their cars; they merely need to know how the touch screen works. Herein lies the success of modifying a new technology by adapting it to the needs of the market. Make it work, and make it simple to use.

Situation 5: The Boom in Electronic Typewriters

Just as electronic calculators had displaced adding machines, electronic typewriters started displacing mechanical typewriters in 1978. Within two years, 200,000 electronic typewriters were sold. In 1984 alone 900,000 units were shipped, and by the end of that year, as many as a third of the eight million office typewriters in use were electronic. In 1985, the shipments exceeded two million units. Here, then, is an innovation that has been readily accepted by the market despite the internal structural adjustments created for the manufacturers.

Remington's first manual (mechanical) typewriter was based on simple engineering: A key was depressed, and a series of levers and springs flipped a bar bearing a single character against an inked ribbon. This created an impression of the letter on the paper in the typewriter carriage. The idea was modified in the electric/electromechanical typewriters, which replaced the manual machines. In electric typewriters, a motor is used to flip the type bars, so that each bar strikes with equal force to give a smooth, printed effect. The next breakthrough was ball technology. Different letters or characters are fixed on a ball; the ball spins, tilts, then presses each character against the ribbon and paper. Meanwhile, electric typewriters had been improved so that the motor could provide extra features, such as automatic carriage return or continuous repetition of a character (such as dashes) when one key is held down.

Then came the electronic typewriters. These machines were based on a totally new technology and required a distinctly different production process, thus creating problems for the manufacturers. While the innovation had to overcome corporate barriers, there was no customer resistance. Major users of the product (secretaries) found it easy to adjust to these machines and enjoyed the increased efficiency.

STRATEGIC CONDITIONS

The M&M strategy succeeds only when certain conditions exist or can be created by the innovative firm. The first condition has to do with technology, the second with market share.

The firm must have access to good R&D facilities.

Keeping Them in the Air

Boeing has constantly urged its engine suppliers—Pratt and Whitney and General Electric—to improve their engines. For instance, the newer engines designed by these suppliers have higher bypass ratios, which in turn reduce fuel requirements and permit heavier payloads to be carried over long distances.

Boeing also designed a larger wing using the new airfoil and structural design technologies. The new wing design allows gross weights of beyond one million pounds, an increase of more than 150,000 pounds over the old. A wider wing span and thicker wing section are now also possible. The new wing design was pioneered on the Boeing 757 and 767 aircraft and proved to be quite successful.

Boeing has also successfully incorporated digital avionics, computer-controlled flight management systems, and electronic instrumentation into their 757 and 767 aircraft. These technologies were successfully transferred to the 747 aircraft as well.

Boeing's design engineers have been equally adept at upgrading the aircraft. For example, Boeing was able to offer their customers aircraft with a stretched upper deck of about 280 inches in length. This nearly doubled the first-class passenger capacity from 24 to 44 seats and could be accommodated with the same engines. Boeing also designed a straight stairway at the aft end of the upper deck, allowing economy coach passengers to board directly through a second door, preventing a traffic pile-up in the first-class section.

The Computers in Command

IBM's top position in the computer industry is a tribute to the firm's perfect reading of the pulse of the marketplace and their ability to respond quickly with a technological breakthrough when threatened.

When IBM struck upon hybrid integrated circuit technology, they were able to develop the revolutionary 360 series, which was far superior to the earlier 1400 series. The new technology was intermediate, between that of discrete components and large-scale integrated circuits. The 360 series also required newer software and permitted the use of higher level languages. IBM had the technical expertise to provide these product improvisations, but the best was yet to come. In the 1400 series, peripherals used on one model of the series could not be used on another. For the 360 series, IBM engineers came up with the standard interface, which allowed the customer to use standardized peripherals across all modes of the series. The freedom to choose from a wide range of peripherals and to switch them across modes proved to be a great benefit to the customers.

IBM was able to develop the 370 series based on the company's new phase 2i bipolar technology. This technology improved the memory of the computers and permitted faster and more reliable processing than the 360 series.

Finally, the 4300 series developed by IBM was the consequence of the company's mastery over the high-memory chip technology. The 64,000-bit chip had a far greater memory than the 370 series and would hold up to 16 times the number of circuits in a 370 model. Further, the cost of producing the chip was a lot less.

IBM's superior R&D expertise has allowed the firm the luxury of using the M&M strategy effectively.

Other Cases

The introduction of mobile phones has been facilitated by the arrival of cellular technology. Only firms that have either developed or bought into the technology have been able to offer the innovation to the marketplace. Otherwise, there would be an expertise barrier that would keep the innovation out of the reach of most potential manufacturers.

In order to computerize road maps in automobiles, the Big Three auto corporations—General Motors, Ford, and Chrysler—have had to obtain access to satellite communications. Further, they have had to draw upon their own technical expertise to devise a glove-compartment-sized video screen. Without access to satellite communications technology and sufficient expertise in automobile design technology, these firms could not have developed innovative computerized graphics that could become an integral part of an individual automobile.

The success of firms in the electronic typewriter business can be attributed not just to their access to electronic technology but to their ability to apply it in the manufacture of typewriters. Firms with good research and development facilities have consistently outdone those without that capacity. A classic example is IBM, with their wide line of electronic typewriters.

The IBM machines needed built-in microprocessor chips, roughly one-quarter of an inch square, which instruct the machine what to do when the keys are depressed. They also incorporated the daisy-wheel technology. The daisy wheel is a symbol-studded printing element, shaped like a wheel with 100 spokes, with a character at the end of each spoke. Typewriters fitted with the daisy wheel hold more characters and can use other wheels with special characters (such as Gothic, foreign, or italic). Finally, electronic typewriters can be programmed to have memory, ranging from the last 10 characters typed to the last two lines.

> The firm must have a large market share in place to migrate customers. Not only does this advantage allow migration to take place easily, but it also spreads the costs of development over a large customer base.

Growing Bigger

Even in the mid-1970s, Boeing had about 63 airline customers in 42 countries operating nine different models of the jumbo 747, from windowless freighters to plush sleepers, from a specially equipped airborne Pentagon command post to the sawed-off special performance machines. Today, Boeing has a large, loyal customer base, who eagerly await Boeing's product developments and who are willing to migrate to the improved versions of the various aircraft models.

Historically, IBM has controlled the market for mainframe computers. IBM products have been accepted as the industry norms, and IBM's quality image has made life difficult for the competition. In fact, several customers have refrained from using systems offered by competitors because they would be exposed to the ridicule of their peers if, even by chance, the non-IBM system they purchased should create problems. IBM has thus enjoyed the benefits of a loyal customer base.

Staying Big

Even though the long distance business has been deregulated for quite some time, AT&T still enjoys a virtual market monopoly despite fierce competition from others, including MCI and U.S. Sprint. Furthermore, AT&T's dominance in of the long distance market seems to be firmly established, even as the communications giant introduces new and innovative digital network services.

In addition, AT&T is upgrading the analog network to a digital network and installing significant amounts of fiber optics for the transmission of information. AT&T will thus be able to offer numerous highly value-added network services to customers who are already loyal to AT&T. For example, despite intense competition and continued regulation by the FCC, AT&T has lost very few large business customers. Big business is looking for new network services, especially for data communication, and AT&T seems to be poised to migrate them to even better innovations.

Systems, Systems, Systems

The innovative firm must adopt a systems selling concept.

IBM sold their customers an entire system: the hardware, the operating system, and the software. Replacements or service could be obtained through IBM's extensive dealer network. Service was also provided to their customers through regular maintenance of the system, as well as in-house training of the systems personnel. Thus, IBM reassured their customers that the company would always be around to help them purchase, install, use, and replace their computer systems. Not only would IBM help out with the hardware but also with peripherals and servicing the whole system. The customers were thus saved the transaction costs of having to deal with several suppliers.

IBM reduced the anxiety of customers who were worried about product obsolescence by giving them the option of leasing the system. If and when a new system was developed, the customer could trade in the lease. There was thus an effective mechanism developed by IBM to migrate and maintain customers who bought or who leased IBM computers.

The Boeing Corporation has also always sold its customers systems of air transport rather than just aircraft. Boeing has taken the initiative to develop all aspects of the aircraft system—the quality of the aircraft engine, the design of the aircraft, the aerodynamic efficiency, the freight-passenger ratio (based on customer needs), the instrumentation in the cockpit, and the servicing and maintenance of the aircraft. Thus, Boeing has an excellent ongoing relationship with their customers, which helps the migration strategy work effectively.

Finally, makers of cellular phones offered their customers the whole package: the phone unit, a power source, an antenna, a cable, antitheft devices (authorized code number), and built-in memory for recalling phone numbers. The customer also had the option of receiving calls or just recording them as they came in. The increasing success of mobile phones can be attributed to a complete system being made available to customers.

CAVEATS

The M&M strategy can be very powerful if market conditions are favorable. You must, however, be aware of two potential dangers. First, eagerness to retain a large share of the market may expose your firm to accusations of monopolistic practice, especially by impotent or frustrated competitors.

The computer industry illustrates this peril very well. In 1969, IBM was charged with attempting to monopolize the computer market. The charges were filed by the Justice Department, and one of the complaints was based on IBM's one-price rental system. IBM was at that time charging rentals only for the hardware and providing service, software, and consultancy free to their customers, effectively preventing competitors from stepping into any of these areas.

In the face of the government challenge, IBM changed their pricing system and began to charge separately for rentals and services. A standard-base contract was drawn up for all equipment that provided for a monthly rental and required a 30-day notice for cancelation. The basic rental covered a fixed number of hours per week of machine use. Additional use would be paid for separately. Service on the rented machines was charged on a separate contract, the price depending on machine use. This unbundling of prices has since become the norm for the computer industry.

Second, the M&M strategy can succeed only if a true win-win situation is created. That is, both the customers and the company must profit from the transaction. This happy condition cannot exist when firms lose sight of the fundamental axiom of success in business: Create value for the customer if you want to make a profit. Product innovation must match customer needs; the market should drive. When the firm is solely technology driven, its products are likely to generate stiff customer resistance over the long haul.

Boeing and IBM again demonstrate how innovations must always consider the customer. Boeing's continuing success with the 747 is, for instance, due to their persistent refinement of the aircraft to meet the two important objectives of customers: increased fuel efficiency and increased payload capacity. In fact, Boeing aircraft have the lowest seat-mile operating cost per passenger in the industry. Thus, not only did the technological innovations improve manufacturing efficiency for Boeing, they also improved the cost effectiveness for consumers: a true win-win situation.

The IBM 4300 series is another innovation that created a win-win situation. For its customers, the 4300 series provided a sevenfold increase in performance for the same price. IBM was also able to enjoy lower costs of producing the chip—a cost saving that they could pass on to their customers and still achieve sufficient profitability and market growth.

An even better story concerns electronic typewriters. To the end users—office secretaries—these machines are sophisticated and convenient devices that have several functional and psychological benefits. First, the new electronic machines look identical to their predecessors—manual and electrical typewriters. Since they do not have the word processor's video-display screen, they are attractive to computer-shy secretaries. Second, the new machines cannot be outtyped by even the most skillful secretary. If the printing mechanism fails to keep pace with the speed of the typist, the memory keeps track of the keys pressed; the machine continues to type and catches up once the typist pauses. The problem of jammed type bars or skipped letters is thus avoided.

Third, the buffer memory makes it easier to correct mistakes. The machine can be instructed to back up, and a correction key can be used to white out the offending characters. Fourth, the machines can be programmed to store several pages of text for future replay. For instance, duplicates of a personal letter can be printed as fast as fresh sheets of paper can be inserted into the typewriter. Fifth, the machine speeds up repetitive typing through automation. An electronic typewriter can be trained to center lines or put a title in the center of a page automatically, or it can make each letter in a word strike twice on the paper for boldface effect. It can hop from blank to blank on purchase-order forms so that a secretary need only fill in the missing information.

Sixth, due to the miniature electronic components used, an electronic typewriter weighs considerably less than its manual or electric counterparts. Seventh, electronic machines reduce chances of error. Features such as spelling dictionaries provide a word-processing function. As a result of this product superiority, electronic typewriters represent a less expensive method (than word processors) of automating the office without changing the work flow. The electronic typewriter thus became a status symbol. There was considerable peer pressure among secretaries to have the best machine, and bosses found it easier and more economical to replace typewriters than secretaries.

From the manufacturers' perspective, electronic technology eliminated the multitudes of levers, springs, gears, and other mechanical parts required by previous technologies. The IBM Selectric, for example, has 2500 parts (fewer than the machines it replaced). The use of electronic circuiting in manufacturing these machines proved to be very cost-effective, and the manufacturers loved the process. The electronic typewriter has succeeded, consequently, because the companies and the customers benefited from the product: a win-win situation.

SUMMARY

Innovations facing only token customer resistance but substantial structural corporate barriers should be brought to market with the Migrate and Maintain strategy. The goal is to retain customers by moving them up to an improved version of the product or service that offers even better relative value. The M&M approach is thus designed to use customer loyalty to repel competitive threats.

Boeing has migrated and maintained airline customers this way, jumbo jets being the latest example. IBM is also famous for this approach in computers. Cellular mobile phones, computers in automobile glove compartments, and electronic typewriters have all applied the M&M strategy successfully as well.

For the strategy to work effectively, the innovating firm must have access to good R&D facilities. A large market share already in place is necessary because it allows development costs to be spread over a bigger base. Firms should adopt a systems selling approach to maintain solid customer relations. Be aware that the M&M strategy can be too successful for the firm's own good. IBM, in particular, has had to fight off monopoly charges because they won too great a market share and kept it. Finally, M&M works when innovations consider the customer's needs; good relations only thrive in the long run in win-win situations.

We have, so far, identified, described, illustrated, and explained how to measure corporate and customer barriers to the marketing of innovations. We then introduced a strategy matrix to help select a marketing approach and investigated the conditions that favored each of those strategies in turn. It is time now to put all of this together in what we hope will be a handy and easy-to-use package. That final task is accomplished in chapter 9.

O'lone, R.G. "Boeing Offers 747 Improvements." *Aviation Week & Space Technology*, April 28, 1980, 24–26.

Petre, P.D. "Who Needs a Smart Typewriter?" *Fortune*, Dec. 29, 1980, 60–64.

Rowan, R. "Business Triumphs of the Seventies [Boeing 747]" *Fortune*, Dec. 31, 1979, 30–34.

"Boeing Looks to Stretching 747 and 767 as 777 Prospects Fade." *Aviation Week & Space Technology*, July 9, 1979, 27.

"Space Age Navigation for the Family Car." *Business Week*, June 10, 1984, 82–84.

"Cutthroat Competition in Mobile Phones." *Fortune*, Feb. 6, 1984.

Intercollegiate Case Clearing House, Boston. 'PCM(A)' [IBM].

"Typewriters: Electronic Fever Hits the Office Market." *Purchasing*, Oct. 22, 1981, 93–94.

9
Putting It All Together

At the outset, we emphasize that this book is not about innovations themselves or the innovative process, but about breaking the barriers that hinder the introduction of innovations into the marketplace. Why is breaking down these barriers such an important aspect of successful management? Because resistance from the corporate side as well as from the customer side is the biggest impediment to the success of new technologies.

Hence, we are confronted with a paradox. Innovations have historically been, and will continue to be, the source of growth and profitability for firms. And yet, both corporations, which need the new products for growth and survival, and customers, who may benefit from them, do not make the transition easily. Innovations tend to impose changes in the accustomed routines of corporations and customers, and this disruption, in turn, generates resistance.

Our book has dealt with this problem by introducing ways to, first, analyze and, then, overcome the resistance inherent in companies and customers so that innovative products and services can be marketed successfully. We will summarize the highlights of our discussion in this concluding chapter.

WHY IS OLD NO LONGER GOLD?

New products and services have become necessary and desirable because of the interplay of four distinct forces that have dominated the social and economic landscape of the 1980s:

1. Changing customers
2. Technological breakthroughs
3. New competition
4. Changing regulation

The key characteristics of each of these forces and the consequent impact on innovations are listed in Table 9.1.

BARRIERS TO INNOVATION

While evolving trends make innovations essential for organizational survival and customer satisfaction, innovating is not easy for either party. Both corporations and customers are confronted with structural barriers that impose a high degree of change or discontinuity. The higher the discontinuity, the higher the resistance to the innovation.

What, then, are these barriers that need to be bypassed or broken for companies to successfully innovate? There are five corporate barriers and five customer barriers that can obstruct the success of innovations. A brief description of each barrier and the solutions to the problems each creates are listed in Tables 9.2 and 9.3.

TABLE 9.1
THE IMPACT OF SOCIAL AND ECONOMIC FORCES ON INNOVATION

Forces	Key Characteristics	Impact (Examples)
	I. Changing Customers	
1. Aging of U.S. population	Health preservation	Health care industry
		Physical fitness centers
		Food industry
	Wealth preservation	Financial services
		Social security systems
	Personal safety & security	Security systems
		Weapons for protection
2. Dual-income families	Time shortage	Retailing institutions (change in working hours)
		Time-responsive services
	Reduced home activities	Boom in child care, restaurants
	Decline of middle class	Premium products
		Market segmentation
3. Single-person households	Loneliness	Singles bars, clubs
		Radio talk shows
	Adult orientation	Television programs
	Individualism	Automobiles, clothing, housing
	II. Technological Breakthroughs	
1. Historical evolution	Progress from mechanical age to electromechanical age to chemical age to electronics and biogenetics ages	All products and services (in mode of production and distribution)

TABLE 9.1 *(Continued)*

Forces	Key Characterisics	Impact (Examples)
2. Temporal progress	Economies of scale (efficiency)	Communications (due to semiconductors, transistors, and computers)
	Economies of scope (versatility)	Microsurgery, fiber optics (due to laser technology)
		Superseed (due to biogenetics)
III. New Competition		
1. Global competition	Relaxation of trade barriers	Increased foreign competition
	Transfer of technology	Increased interdependence among nations
	Increasing number of global mergers, acquisitions, and strategic alliances (e.g., GM–Toyota, Nestle–Carnation)	All industry players have to react to maintain status quo
		All the above necessitates adaption of product/service to *new* markets
2. Productivity drive	Increased human productivity	Computer-aided manufacturing
	Increased plant productivity	Office automation
		Local area networks
		Integrated manufacturing
3. Quality assurance	Shift from low price–low quality goods to value	Emulation of Japanese methods

TABLE 9.1 *(Continued)*

Forces	Key Characteristics	Impact (Examples)
	IV. Changing Regulation	
1. Deregulation of industry	Change in competitive structure	Firms in service industries such as telecommunications, airlines, and banking have to adapt to survive
2. Technical standards	Ensures compatibility and comparability of competitive offerings	Telephone-computer link governed by Integrated Services Defined Networks (ISDN)
3. Safety standards	Consumer protection	Drugs and chemicals Foods

TABLE 9.2
CORPORATE BARRIERS TO INNOVATION

Barriers	Sources	Solutions
1. Expertise	Over-specialization, technology-driven innovations EXAMPLES Surgery (limited to field of specialization, such as eye surgery) Steel production (not transferable to plastics) USCI's failure in DBS TV IBM's failure in copying machines	Skunk works; e.g., IBM's personal computer Research alliances; e.g., videotex services Acquisitions; e.g., Sears' acquisition of Dean Witter and Coldwell Banker for financial services

TABLE 9.2 *(Continued)*

Barriers	Sources	Solutions
2. Operations	Changes required in materials procurement, manufacturing, worker training EXAMPLES OF DIFFICULT TRANSITIONS Large- to small-car manufacture Wines to wine coolers Metals to plastics in appliances	Separate operations; e.g., GM's Saturn plant Modified operations; e.g., robots in auto manufacture
3. Resources	Low capital reserves and borrowing power EXAMPLES Failure of Freddie Laker's airline ITT abandons digital switch development Miller's success in Lite beer	License agreements; e.g., Sony's 8mm videocamera Consortiums; e.g., smart house project Venture capital
4. Regulation	Regulation from government, self-regulation within industry, patents EXAMPLES American Medical Association FDA's approval of drugs, irradiation of foods Interstate banking laws Public Utility Commission regulation of local phone companies	Abolish the regulation by legislation; e.g., airlines industry Shift regulatory jurisdiction; e.g., morality standards Reorganize the firm to counter regulatory requirements; e.g., banking

TABLE 9.2 *(Continued)*

Barriers	Sources	Solutions
5. Market access	Lack of access to customers because of distribution strength or entrenchment of competitors EXAMPLES Customer loyalty to IBM in computers Coca-Cola and Pepsi control soft drink outlets Bell Operating Companies control access to homes and offices International trade barriers	Align with the dominant vendor; e.g., Michelin tires Develop your own distribution network; e.g., Tupperware Use a pull strategy for the products/services; e.g., Japanese electronics in India

TABLE 9.3
CUSTOMER BARRIERS TO INNOVATION

Barriers	Sources	Solutions
1. Usage	Incompatible with customers' existing work flows, practices, habits EXAMPLES Software not compatible with IBM hardware Robots in the factory Carpooling Tofu as a protein substitute	Develop a systems perspective; e.g., dishwashers Integrate the innovation into other activities or products; e.g., computer peripherals Make innovation mandatory through governmental legislation; e.g., lead free gasoline

TABLE 9.3 *(Continued)*

Barriers	Sources	Solutions
2. Value	Low performance–price ratio EXAMPLES ATM banking machines RCA video disc player Video conferencing Corfam (substitute for leather)	Provide increased performance value; e.g., electronic calculators Use cost cutting and pass on savings to customers; e.g., digital watches Add value to innovation by product repositioning; e.g., Campbell's soup
3. Risk	Economic loss, physical danger, and performance uncertainty EXAMPLES Irradiated foods Sugar substitutes (saccharin) Consumer electronics AT&T long distance service	Free trials; e.g., herbicides Testimonials; e.g., books System packaging; e.g., imitation cheese
4. Tradition	Social norms and corporate culture EXAMPLES Computerized dating Replacement of personal secretaries by word processing centers Plastic instead of glass or metal	Understand and respect cultural tradition Educate the market; e.g., modern agriculture Use change agents; e.g., office equipment

Measuring the Barriers

TABLE 9.3 *(Continued)*

Barriers	Sources	Solutions
5. Image	Negative associations, sterotyped thinking, taboos EXAMPLES Indian machine tools Prunes Motorcycles associated with gangsterism in the 1950s Lawyers (ambulance chasers)	Make fun of the image; e.g., motorcycles Create a new image; e.g., wine coolers Make positive associations; e.g., Indian machine tools

MEASURING THE BARRIERS

In chapter 4, we illustrated how to measure the strength of each of the five corporate barriers and five customer barriers and thus calculate the extent and nature of the resistance to a particular innovation. Focusing on the telecommunications industry, we organized innovations into one of four classes according to the combined power of the corporate and the customer barriers (see Figure 9.1).

This classification schema is very useful because it allows a firm to explicitly examine the structural barriers an innovation faces from the corporation as well as from the customers. The 4x4 schema also forms the basis for a marketing strategies matrix, which is a tool for selecting the mode of attack that will be most likely to break or circumvent the barriers and create new product success. Every innovation meets with different levels of resistance. The choice of an appropriate strategy for introducing the innovation to the marketplace will, in turn, depend on the degree of corporate resistance as well as the degree of customer resistance (see Figure 9.2).

Figure 9.1. Classification of telecommunications innovations

Customer barriers / Corporate barriers matrix:

	Customer barriers High	Customer barriers Low
Corporate barriers High	Videotex / ISDN	Digital centrex / Cellular mobile phones
Corporate barriers Low	Electronic mail / Lifeline service	800 Number service / Custom calling service

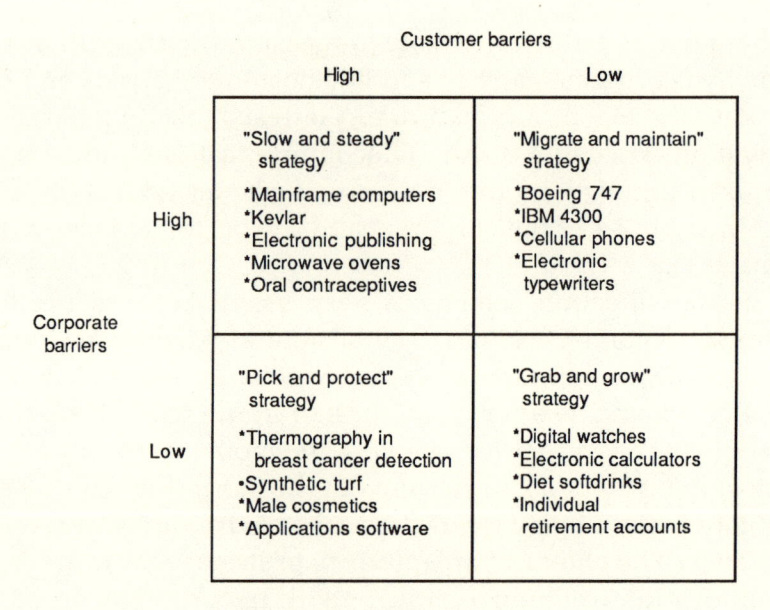

Figure 9.2. Strategy matrix

	Customer barriers High	Customer barriers Low
Corporate barriers High	"Slow and steady" strategy *Mainframe computers *Kevlar *Electronic publishing *Microwave ovens *Oral contraceptives	"Migrate and maintain" strategy *Boeing 747 *IBM 4300 *Cellular phones *Electronic typewriters
Corporate barriers Low	"Pick and protect" strategy *Thermography in breast cancer detection *Synthetic turf *Male cosmetics *Applications software	"Grab and grow" strategy *Digital watches *Electronic calculators *Diet softdrinks *Individual retirement accounts

THE SLOW AND STEADY STRATEGY

The Slow and Steady (S&S) strategy entails introducing a new product or service on a very selective basis to the market.

> The S&S strategy attempts to access several layers/groups of customers in a slow but steady succession, beginning with high value segments and moving on to segments of declining value.

A firm resorting to the S&S strategy must therefore be able to list, in order of importance, customer needs that can be catered to by the innovation. DuPont was able to do this effectively for Kevlar, the miracle substitute for steel. Kevlar went slowly but steadily through several customer groups, beginning with the aerospace and airline industry, and progressing to the markets for bulletproof armor, luxury boats, power transmission cables, automobiles, and other industrial applications. IBM successfully marketed its first mainframe computer by focusing initially on the *Fortune* 500 firms and the large government agencies, before moving on to the midsize and small firms.

> A firm adopting the S&S strategy must make sure that it is protected by high entry barriers.

DuPont spent several million dollars in developing Kevlar. Its research expertise and financial resources provided sufficient deterrents to competitive entry. Further, DuPont took care to protect its technological breakthroughs by patenting. Well guarded by these entry barriers, DuPont could afford to go slow in market development.

> The S&S strategy is designed to allow quick recovery of the high costs of production and R&D for the innovation.

With the increasing costs of new product development, especially in the R&D and production stages, cost recovery has become a major concern for innovating firms. The S&S strategy facilitates cost recovery by going after the most lucrative customers first because these customers are willing to pay a premium to use the product. Recall the high prices of the first personal computers or the original high subscription fees for cable television compared to what they are today. DuPont similarly used a premium pricing strategy to market Kevlar to the high value segments—in this case, the aerospace industry.

> Customers are not in a position to evaluate the performance of the innovation against a substitute, especially if the innovation is based on a new technology.

The first duplicating machine developed by Xerox, vasectomy designed as a radical new male contraception method, and the first disposable diaper are examples of innovations that were totally new to the customer. These products had no substitutes based on a similar, existing technology; thus, there was no comparison for the customer to make prior to accepting the innovation.

> The S&S strategy should always begin with the leading edge of the market.

In the corporate world, the leading edge is represented by firms with sophisticated technology, often the *Fortune* 100 companies. For customer products and services, the leading-edge customers are the opinion leaders: the young, affluent, mobile individuals, who have both the willingness to try something new and the ability to pay for it.

There are two major caveats that an innovating firm should be aware of before instituting the S&S strategy:

1. There must be a sufficient number of customers with a high usage potential for the innovation.

2. These customers should be able and willing to pay the higher price to use the innovation.

The initial market failure of lead free gasoline illustrates these dangers quite effectively.

THE GRAB AND GROW STRATEGY

The Grab and Grow (G&G) strategy is ideal when an innovation faces low corporate barriers and low customer barriers. The G&G strategy involves introducing the innovation on a mass market basis. The innovating firm seeks to offer the innovation to a large number of receptive customers, thus capitalizing on an early entry into the market. The company then builds its experience faster than its competitors by grabbing as much of the market as possible and growing rapidly to reach a formidable competitive position.

Examples of innovations that have succeeded in the marketplace through the G&G strategy are plentiful. The digital watch, the electronic dashboards in autos, and diet soft drinks gained quick market share for those firms that adopted the G&G approach. For the G&G strategy to be effective, however, the firm offering the innovation must have certain conditions in its favor.

> The firm must have access to the experience curve or the headstart benefits, and must focus on overall cost advantage.

Texas Instruments (TI) obtained their cost advantage in producing electronic calculators from two sources. First, they used low-cost production facilities in countries like Spain. Second, TI automated their testing procedures and expanded their production so rapidly that the unit cost of the product dropped from the sheer volume of production. The success of TI's strategy became obvious when competitors such as Bowman and Hewlett-Packard followed in their footsteps.

> The firm must have a strong distribution system at its disposal.

When the telephone equipment market was deregulated in 1985, GE was able to make quick inroads because the company had a well developed distribution system already in place.

Texas Instruments' success in the electronic calculator market was also aided by an excellent dealer network. Their dealers were a highly motivated group. Since they were protected by TI from sudden price changes, these faithful dealers contributed to the success of TI's Grab and Grow strategy.

Japanese automakers made their entry into the U.S. markets by borrowing the distribution network of General Motors and Ford. The Japanese already had a cost advantage; what they needed was rapid access to the market; they achieved this by convincing U.S. dealers to sell their products to families as second cars.

> The management of a firm must be willing to take risks for long-term payoffs.

At the risk of never being able to recover their investment, Texas Instruments achieved price leadership in the electronic calculator market. By constantly announcing lower priced models, TI preempted competitors' sales and enjoyed a large customer base. The strategy began to pay off once a sufficiently huge sales volume was obtained.

> A firm must be capable of upgrading its products in the long run.

Witness the evolution of Apple's personal computer. First there was the Apple II, targeted toward users in businesses, homes, and schools. With increasing competitive pressure, the Macintosh emerged with graphic capabilities and higher memory. Then came Lisa and Lisa 2, further improvements in the product line. Apple thus had to constantly upgrade their products to keep their hold in the market.

In adopting the G&G strategy, a firm should remember the following caveats:

1. (a) It should not overestimate the size of the market. (b) It should have access to experience curve benefits, which cannot be imitated. (c) It should not underestimate the competition. Texas Instruments failed in the personal computer market clearly because it was guilty of ignoring all three warnings.
2. A firm should realize under what circumstances the G&G strategy will be appropriate. G.D. Searle's failure to use a G&G strategy for Aspartame could prove detrimental in the long run.

THE PICK AND PROTECT STRATEGY

When an innovation does not generate much structural corporate resistance but does face high customer barriers, the Pick and Protect (P&P) strategy is appropriate. An innovating firm has to pick the right application for which the innovation creates the highest customer value. Since corporate barriers are low, competitive entry is a distinct possibility. Hence, the firm needs to protect its customer base from competitors.

Monsanto's synthetic turf and Vectra International's application of thermography for breast cancer detection are examples of innovations where the P&P strategy has worked effectively. For P&P to be effective, a few favorable conditions are necessary.

> The innovation has to be customized to respond to a segment's needs as closely as possible.

Vectra International Corporation was successful in applying thermography for the detection of breast cancer. Until thermography was used for this application, mammography was the only alternative. However, mammography uses an X-ray technique, and X rays can be a radiation hazard for women with a family history of breast cancer. Vectra International developed a special technique based on liquid crystal technology to help detect breast cancer lumps using body temperature differences. By improving the chances of detecting the cancer, Vectra International picked a lucrative segment to serve.

Similarly, software manufacturers have survived by picking one of three niches in which to operate: (1) applications software, (2) utility software, or (3) systems control software. Within each niche, the software manufacturers develop packages to suit each customer's specific needs.

> Once a firm picks a niche, it must be aggressive and seek to protect it, or else competitors may decide to grab a piece of the action.

Once Vectra International opened the market for thermography (to detect breast cancer), they proceeded to protect their position. First, Vectra set up a control laboratory of trained technicians who could receive and analyze photographs. Second, they created a classification system for cancer victims, which could be used as the benchmark for analysis. With these unique benefits, Vectra sought to develop distinctive strengths that would defend the market against competitors.

Two caveats that an innovating firm needs to be aware of in using the P&P strategy are:

1. Unless it has the advantage of being the early entrant in a segment, the innovating firm may have already lost out to other companies that made the first move.
2. A firm should not underestimate competitors' ability to attack and move into the niche.

THE MIGRATE AND MAINTAIN STRATEGY

When an innovation meets only low customer resistance, but is confronted with high corporate barriers, the Migrate and Maintain (M&M) strategy is the correct selection. In this approach, the innovating firm maintains its customer base by migrating the customers to an upgraded version of the product. The customers, who are quite satisfied with the current version of the product, are only too happy to get something even better.

Examples of innovations that have succeeded on the basis of the M&M strategy are the Boeing 747 aircraft and the IBM 4300 series of computers. But for the M&M strategy to work well, a firm must ensure that certain conditions are satisfied.

> The firm must have access to good R&D facilities.

Boeing has been able to upgrade their aircraft through the labors of an excellent R&D team. The Boeing R&D team designed a larger wing span, incorporated computer technology into the instrumentation and the flight management systems of the aircraft, and improved the fuel efficiency.

IBM's command of the computer marketplace can also be attributed to the technological breakthroughs achieved by the company's research team. These include the hybrid integrated circuit technology, computer peripherals compatible across all models of a series, phase 2i bipolar technology, and the 64,000-bit chip, to name a few.

> The firm must have a large market share in place to be able to migrate its customers.

Even as early as the mid-1970s, Boeing had about 63 customers in 42 countries operating nine different models of the jumbo jet. Similarly, IBM has always had a strong hold on the market for mainframe computers and has generally been accepted as establishing the industry norm. Finally, the Big Three of the U.S. automobile industry—GM, Ford, Chrysler—have been able to build options into their automobiles and offer them to customers as standard features because of market dominance.

The firm must adopt a systems selling concept.

IBM sells customers an active system: hardware, operating system, software, installation, maintenance, after-sales service, and even replacement. Similarly, Boeing offers its customers a system of air transport: a high quality engine, a design that provides aerodynamic efficiency, a freight–passenger ratio to suit customer needs, superior instrumentation, and service and maintenance of the aircraft when required.

Innovative firms considering the M&M strategy must bear two caveats in mind:

1. Eagerness to retain a large share of the market may expose the firm to accusations of monopolistic practice, especially by impotent or frustrated competitors.
2. Innovations must meet customer needs so that a true win-win situation is created for both the innovating firm and the customers.

EPILOGUE

Change is destabilizing. It disrupts the smooth routine that has become an intrinsic part of the day-to-day activities of corporations and customers alike. Innovations tend to impose change on both the customer and the corporation. The higher the degree of change, the higher the discontinuity or disruption, and, consequently, the higher the resistance.

Epilogue

The key, therefore, is to understand the extent of change created by an innovation. Firms must then analyze and measure the strength of the five corporate barriers and five customer barriers that naturally spring up to challenge their innovation. Once a firm evaluates the barriers faced by the new product or service, it can decide on an appropriate strategy that will successfully take the innovation to market. Abandoning an innovation out of fear of the high degree of change is not, therefore, the solution. Understanding barriers to change, and then managing them, is the answer. Break the shackles of routine, break the barriers to innovation, and you are on the road to success.

Index

Ace Hardware, 48
Acquisitions, 21, 38–39, 49, 74, 220, 221
Activision, 177
Adaptability, 5
Additives, 52
Adult life-styles, 15
Advertising, 38, 47, 51, 59, 76, 84, 156
Aerospace industry, 228
Aetna Life and Casualty Company, 161
Affluent class, 14
Aging, 7–12, 14, 16, 82, 219
Agricultural society, 5
Agriculture, 50, 51, 75–76, 92, 224
Agriculture, Department of (USDA), 89
Air bags, 63–64, 158
Aircraft industry, 149, 212
Airline industry, 24, 57, 88, 221, 222, 227
Alberto-Culver, 180
Alliances, 58
   economic, 21
   research, 37–38, 221
   strategic, 21, 100, 105
Alnet, 46, 172, 173
American Bar Association, 50
American Express Company, 38, 76
American Home Builders Association, 38

American Medical Association, 50, 222
AMP Corporation, 38
Animal feed, 92
Antitrust violations, 50
Apple Computers, 36, 80, 176, 230
Applications, 183, 231
Arrow Shirts, 83
Arthur D. Little, 32
Aspartame, 80, 179, 233. See also
   Nutrasweet
AT&T:
   computers, 36, 67
   deregulation, 46, 172–173, 210–211
   divestiture, 53–54, 81
   entry barrier, 157
   expertise barrier, 33, 119, 124
   leading edge strategy, 89
   research alliances, 38
   resource barrier, 101
   risk, 224
   value barrier, 72
Automatic teller machines (ATMs), 72–73, 88, 102, 224
Automation, 231
   factory, 23, 42, 67, 107
   office, 22, 39, 74, 85, 89, 107, 214, 220

Index

Automation (*Continued*)
 warehouse, 44
Automobile industry:
 global competition in, 21, 67, 174–175
 market access, 125
 Migrate and Maintain strategy, 204–206, 209, 234
 operations barrier, 40, 42–43, 224
 Pick and Protect strategy, 188–189, 194–195
 safety, 63–64
Avon Cosmetics, 58

Baby boom, 8, 9, 16
Balance of payments, 56
Banking, 52–53, 72–73, 87–88, 90, 100, 102, 103, 170, 221, 222
Bankruptcy, 46, 74
Barriers, see Individual barriers by name
 entry, 156–157, 227
 expertise, 31, 32–39
 image, 90–94
 market access, 55–59
 operations, 31, 39–44
 regulation, 50–55, 79
 resource, 44–50
 tradition, 84–90
 usage, 66–71
 value, 71–78
Bayer Aspirin, 76
Beatrice, 38, 39
Beef industry, 8–9, 87
Beer industry, 46, 94
Bell Laboratories, 32
Bell Operating Companies (BOCs), 53, 81, 101, 110, 172–173, 223
Bell System, 50, 54, 128, 130
Betty Crocker, 88
Bioengineering, 37
Biogenetic age, 18
Biogenetics, 21, 37, 219, 220
Birth control, 89, 148, 155–156, 159
Boeing Corporation, 57, 200–201, 207, 210, 212, 213, 233
Borrowing power, 45, 99, 222
Bowmar, 172, 230
Branch banking, 52, 54
Brand names, 76
Brazil, 5, 21, 75, 91, 171
Break-even point, 166

Buppies, 90
Burroughs Corporation, 188
Business hours, 13
Buying habits, 71

Cable communications, 158
Calculators, *see* Electronic calculators
Campbell Soup Company, 78, 224
Canada, 56, 180
Cancer detection, *see* Thermography
Capital, 31, 99, 146
Capital infusion, 11
Capital-intensive services, 146
Carnation, 38, 220
Casio, 77, 167
Cellular telephones, 71, 123–128, 137, 203–204, 209, 212
Century 21, 48
Change agents, 89–90, 224
Cheap goods, 23
Chemical age, 18, 219
Chemical industry, 37, 51, 65, 144, 186
Chiclet chewing gum, 22
China, 5, 87, 89, 187
Chrysler Corporation, 21, 43, 70, 168–169, 195, 204, 234
Citicorp, 87–88
Citizen (watches), 77, 167
Clinique cosmetics, 58
Coca-Cola, 9, 55, 76, 169, 172, 223
Coffee industry, 9–10
Colgate, 76
Commodore Computers, 178, 192
Communications technology, 105, 203, 220
Competition:
 AT&T, 211
 in automobile industry, 126
 in computer industry, 210
 and efficiency, 24
 in electronic publishing, 146
 entry barriers and, 156
 foreign, 42, 56, 67
 global, 20–22
 and innovation, 6, 218
 market access, 223
 Migrate and Maintain strategy, 212
 vs. monopolies, 90
 Pick and Protect stragety, 196
 price/promotion, 20, 125, 171, 173
 regulating, 50

Index

Competitive advantage, 4, 157, 165, 174, 192
Computer industry, 35–37, 67, 77, 210, 212, 221
Computers:
  as change agents, 90
  efficiency, 18–19
  potential, 65, 67, 161, 230
  resistance to, 74, 80, 103
  smart house technology, 37–38, 48
  software development, 188
  technology transfer, 21
  value barrier, 111
COMSAT General Corporation, 161
Confidentiality, 111, 112
Consolidation, 20, 54
Consortiums, 48–49, 222
Consultative Committee on International Telecommunications and Telegraphs (CCITT), 49, 104
Consumer advocates, 65
Consumer demand, 10, 41
Consumer electronics industry, 73, 80, 224
Consumer protection, 223
Consumer response, 41, 66
Consumer sector, 5
Consumption, 15
Contact lenses, 75–76
Convenience, 72, 103
Copyrights, 188. See also Patents
Corfam, 75
Corporate culture, 49, 107, 112, 122, 131, 224
Corporate growth, 139
Cosmetics, male, 187, 193–194
Cost advantage, 171, 174, 229, 230
Cost-cutting measures, 146, 171, 224
Cost efficiencies, 143, 171
Cost-plus-margin system, 165
Cost recovery, 158–159, 227
Cost reduction, 31, 173
Cranberry sauce, 86
Crisis management, 107
Cultural discontinuity, 84. See also Discontinuity
Cultural traditions, 87–88, 99, 224. See also Tradition barrier
Cumberland Packing Company, 180
Custom calling services (CCS), 132–136, 137

Customer acceptance, 192
Customer base, 201, 210, 233
Customer behavior patterns, 163
Customer complaints, 189
Customer loyalty, 199, 223
Customer needs, 6, 16, 33, 41, 139, 149, 163
Customers, changing, 6–16, 218, 219
Customer service, 13
Customization, 189

Dart Industries, 39
Data communication, 211
Data General, 67, 77
Debt-to-equity ratio, 45
Defense, Department of, 205
Demand-driven innovation, 9
Demographic pattern, 10
Demographic shift, 12, 78
Demographic trends, 7
  aging, 7–12, 14, 16, 82, 219
  dual-income families, 12–14, 219
  single-person households, 14–16, 219
Denmark, 21–22
Deregulation, 24, 71, 106, 125, 173, 178, 210, 221, 230
Design engineering, 39
Developing nations, 5, 10, 21, 148
Diesel engines, 34, 188–189, 194–195
Diet beverages, 169–170
Digital centrex, 117–122, 137
Digital Equipment Corporation (DEC), 71, 77, 188
Direct-broadcast-by satellite (DBS), 29
Direct marketing, 38, 58
Discontinuity, 84, 139, 143, 144, 184, 218, 234
Discounts, 71
Discretionary recreation, 15
Dishwashers, 41, 70
Distribution, 51, 145
Distribution channels, 30, 58, 101, 125
Distribution network, 162, 223
Distribution problems, 99
Distribution systems, 9, 13, 42, 44, 173, 230
Distribution technology, 130
Divestiture, 53–54, 172
Downstreaming, 43
Drucker, Peter, 6
Dual-income families, 12–14, 219

Index

DuPont, 74–75, 144–145, 154, 156, 159, 227. *See also* Kevlar

E-com, 109
Economic alliances, 21
Economic gap, 18
Economic risk, 78, 80, 127, 131, 143
Economy of scale, 17, 80, 171, 177, 181, 220
Economy of scope, 17, 220
EDS, 39
Education, 88–89, 102, 178, 188, 224
Efficiency, 17, 24, 31, 32, 34, 44, 111, 167, 171, 207, 213, 220
Efficiency curve, 40
Electric cars, 69
Electromechanical age, 17–18, 219
Electromechanical technology, 143
Electronic age, 18, 219
Electronic calculators, 170–171, 206, 224
Electronic communications, 18
Electronic games, 100
Electronic mail, 108–112, 137, 161
Electronic publishing, 145–147, 154–156, 157
Electronics business, 143, 224
Electronic shopping, 100
Electronic technology, 157, 171, 209, 215
Electronic typewriters, 206–207, 209, 214
Eli Lily, 53
Employment, 10
Employment-based income, 11
Endorsements, 82–83
Energy conservation, 89
England, 53, 88
Entrepreneurial companies, 46
Entry barriers, 156–157, 227
Environmental challenges, 44–59
  market access barrier, 55–59
  regulation barrier, 50–55
  resource barrier, 44–50
Environmental Protection Agency (EPA), 50, 162
Esmark, 38
Ethics, 50
European Common Market, 21
Experience, 171–173
Experience curve, 32, 80, 171, 174, 177, 178, 229, 231
Experimentation, 32
Expertise, investment in, 143, 227

Expertise barrier:
  cellular phones, 124, 209
  custom calling services, 132–133
  electronic mail, 109
  electronic publishing, 146
  lifeline services, 113
  microwave ovens, 147
  office technology, 118–119
  overspecialization, 98, 221
  specialization trap, 31, 32–39
  telecommunications industry, 104–105
  thermography, 185
  toll-free services, 128–129
  videotex, 100
Exxon, 39

Factory automation, 23, 42, 67, 107
Federal Aviation Administration (FAA), 50, 201
Federal Communications Commission (FCC), 123, 125, 211
Federal Express, 57
Federal Trade Commission (FTC), 50, 51
Fertility rate, 7
Fiber optics, 104, 105, 211, 220
Field testing, 70
Financial planning, 11
Financial services industry, 11, 52, 219, 221
Firestone Tires, 58
Fitness, 7, 219
Flavor enhancers, 52
Flexibility, 170
Food and Drug Administration (FDA), 52, 53, 179, 180, 185, 222
Food industry, 38, 48, 51–52, 69, 93, 181, 219, 221
Food preservation, 52, 79
Ford Motor Company, 21, 174, 195, 204, 209, 230, 234
Foreign competition, 42, 67, 220. *See also* Global competition
Fortune 500 companies, 143, 160, 227
France, 56, 195
Franchising, 48
Free trial, 82, 224
French National Institution of Health and Medical Research, 195
Friedman, Milton, 10
Funds transfer, 52, 100

Index   241

Gallo Wines, 94
General Agreements on Trade and Tarriffs (GATT), 21
General Electric, 38, 41, 83, 173, 178, 207, 230
General Foods, 9, 38, 180
General Motors:
    alliances, 58
    global competition, 21, 174, 220, 230
    market dominance, 234
    mergers, 39
    Migrate and Maintain strategy, 204, 209
    Pick and Protect strategy, 188, 195, 196
    separate operations, 42, 222
    specialization trap, 34
Geographic dispersion, 161
Geostar Corporation, 205
Germany, 91
Gillette, 76
Global competition, 20–22, 98, 220. *See also* Foreign competition
Goodrich, B.F., 58
Goodyear Tire and Rubber Company, 58, 153
Grab and Grow strategy, 165–182, 229–231
Growth, 5, 47, 139, 213
GTE, 46, 173

Health care:
    research alliances, 37
    resource barrier, 47
    safety standards, 26
    societal needs, 7
    World Health Organization (WHO), 88–89
Health care industry, 53, 54, 81, 84, 219
Health maintenance organizations (HMOs), 47
Health preservation, 7–10, 219
Herd mentality, 81
Hewlett-Packard, 67, 172, 188, 230
Hilton Hotel Corporation, 42
Hitachi, 47
Holding companies, 54
Honda, 92, 94, 175
Honeywell, 71
Huppies, 90

IBM:
    alliances, 58
    and competition, 50, 56
    and computer industry, 67, 71, 74, 80, 176, 188, 196, 212
    customer loyalty, 223
    discontinuity, 143
    entry barrier, 157, 227
    expertise barrier, 32
    image, 94, 210
    innovation at, 3–5
    leading-edge marketing, 89, 161
    market access, 188
    market dominance, 195, 208
    Migrate and Maintain strategy, 201–203, 208–209, 210, 233
    pricing strategy, 201, 213
    risk, 82
    skunk works, 35, 223
    software development, 192
    systems selling, 211
    tradition barrier, 84–85
IGA Supermarkets, 48
Image, 48, 94, 210
Image barrier:
    cellular phones, 127
    custom calling services, 135
    digital centrex, 122
    electronic calculators, 171
    electronic mail, 112
    lifeline services, 117
    microwave ovens, 147
    negative, 99, 148, 171, 225
    oral contraceptives, 148
    as psychological block, 90–94, 99
    telecommunications industry, 108
    thermography, 186
    toll-free services, 131–132
    videotex, 103–104
Income, 10, 13
India, 5, 21, 22, 59, 75, 87, 89, 91, 187, 223, 225
Individualistic life-styles, 15, 219
Individual Retirement Accounts (IRAs), 170
Industrial Revolution, 16, 17
Industrial sector, 5, 74
Industrial society, 5, 17–18
Industry growth, 47
Industry life cycle, 19
Inflation, 10, 170
Information age technologies, 25

Index

Innovation drive, 5, 27
Integrated Services Defined Network (ISDN), 25, 27, 104–108, 137, 221
Integration, 70–71, 101, 104
Interactive education, 100
Interactive entertainment, 100
Interbanking, 52
Interest rates, 10
International Telecommunications Union, 49
International trade, 21, 56, 80, 223
Interstate banking, 52
Intrapreneuring, 5
Invention, 16, 51
  of image, 94
Investment-related income, 11
Irridiation, 51–52, 79, 147, 222, 224
Italy, 75, 171
ITT, 33, 46, 105, 224

Japan:
  automobile industry, 21, 174, 220, 230
  banking, 52, 72
  consumer electronics industry, 73, 223
  debt-to-equity ratio, 45
  image barrier, 91
  market boundaries, 20
  marketing, 59
  price competition, 77, 166
  quality assurance, 23, 220
  trade barriers, 56, 88
Jobs, Steve, 36
Justice, Department of (DOJ), 50, 212
Just-in-time concept, 23

Kevlar, 144–145, 149–154, 156, 159, 227
Keynesian economics, 10
Knight Ridder Services, 101, 157
Kodak, 40
Korea, 20, 21, 56, 91, 94
Kraft, 39, 56

Labeling, 51
Labor-intensive services, 81, 146
Laker, Freddie, 45–46, 222
Laser technology, 19, 43, 220
Law and order, 12
Lead free gasoline, 71, 162
Leading-edge marketing, 89, 160–161, 228
Learning curve, 17, 35

Legislation, 71, 223
Liability, 81
License agreements, 47–48, 222
Lifeline service, 112–117, 137
Life-styles, 15, 116, 135, 219
Literacy, 89, 148
Loneliness, 15
L'Oreal, 76
Low-income class, 14
Luxembourg, 55

McDonald's, 48, 76
Machine tools industry, 91
Magazines, 15
Mail order, 51
Malaysia, 172
Male cosmetics, see Cosmetics, male
Malpractice, 81
Manufacturing, 23, 39, 42, 77, 99, 124, 145, 171, 177, 185, 222
Mariott Hotels, 42
Market acceptance, 156
Market access, 31, 120–121, 185, 188
Market access barrier:
  cellular phones, 125–126
  custom calling services, 134
  electronic mail, 110
  electronic publishing, 146
  as environmental challenge, 55–59, 99
  lifeline services, 115
  oral contraceptives, 148
  soft drink industry, 223
  telecommunications industry, 106
  toll-free services, 130
  trade barriers, 225
  videotex, 101–102
Market boundaries, 22, 25
Market development, 139, 141, 150, 181, 204, 227
Market dominance, 234
Market-driven innovation, 33, 35, 40
Market entry, 165, 229
Market gap, 7, 12, 13
Market growth, 213
Marketing, 48, 59, 225
Market opportunities, 146
Market penetration, 158, 196
Market presence, 195
Market segments, 14, 78, 143, 149, 151, 172, 189, 192, 196, 219, 232

Index

Market share, 3, 55, 58, 166, 172, 173, 178, 181, 207, 210, 212
Market size, 47, 177, 231
Marlboro cigarettes, 94
Materials procurement, 39, 48, 99, 222
Matsushita, 45, 47
Mattel toys, 177
Maxicare, 47
Mazda, 21, 175
MCI, 46, 110, 161, 172, 173, 211
Measurement procesures, 97–136, 225–226
Mechanical age, 17, 219
Mennen, 76
Mergers, 21, 38–39, 49, 74, 220
"Me too" brand names, 76
Mexico, 171, 172
Michelin Tires, 58, 223
Microwave ovens, 147–148, 155
Middle class, 14
Migrate and Maintain strategy, 199–217, 233–234
Migration, 120, 199, 210, 211, 212
Miller beer, 47, 94, 224
Ministry of International Trade and Industries (MITI), 47
Minivans, 70
Minnesota Mining and Manufacturing Company, 38
Mitsubishi, 21, 45, 175
Mitsui, 45
Modified operations, 42–44, 222
Monaco, 55
Monetary policies, 10
Monopolies, 24, 50, 51, 64, 90, 210, 212
Monsanto, 186–187, 193, 231
Morale, 44
Morality, 54, 222
Mortality rate, 7, 190
Motorcycles, 92–93, 225
Motorola, 124
Mrs. Field's Cookies, 35

Nabisco, 38
Nader, Ralph, 63
National banking, 52
Natural resources, 86
NCR, 67
Negative image, 99, 148, 171, 225
Negative population base, 7

Nestle, 38, 220
Net worth, 10
New Federalism, 54
New products, 158, 161, 204, 227
Newspapers, 15, 101, 155
Nissan, 175
North American Phillips, 177
Northern Telecom, 33, 119
NutraSweet, 80, 170, 179. See also Aspartame

Occupational safety, 50
Ocean Spray, 86
Office automation, 22, 39, 74, 85, 89, 107, 214, 220
Oki, 124
Olivetti, 37
Operational changes, 146
Operational facilities, 186
Operations, 42–44, 222
Operations barrier:
  cellular phones, 124
  custom calling services, 133
  digital centrex, 119
  electronic mail, 109
  lifeline services, 113–114
  manufacturing, 99, 222
  microwave ovens, 147
  overspecialization, 39
  soft drink industry, 169
  specialization trap, 31, 39–44
  telecommunications industry, 105
  toll-free services, 129
  videotex, 100–101
Opinion leaders, 89, 161, 227
Oral contraceptives, 148, 155
Original equipment manufacturer (OEM), 83
Overspecialization, 39, 98, 221
Oversupply, 178

Pacific Bell, 102
Packaging, 40, 51, 67, 83–84, 85, 148, 224
Pampers, 160
Patents, 51, 157, 180, 181, 222, 227
Pension plans, 11
Pepsi-Cola, 55, 169, 172, 223
Per capita consumption, 15
Performance, 77, 79, 159, 171
Performance–price index, 3–4

Index

Performance–price ratio, 9, 52, 71, 80, 99, 175, 197, 201, 202, 224
Performance–price superiority, 78
Performance–price value, 4, 74, 102, 111
Performance uncertainty, 99, 143, 145, 147, 224
Permanent income, 10
Personal communication, 112
Pharmaceutical industry, 32, 37, 51, 53, 76, 87, 148, 221
Philip Morris, 38, 47
Physical risk, 79
Pick and Protect strategy, 183–198, 231–232
Place, convenience, 72
Plastics industry, 85, 173
Population decline, 7
Pornography, 54
Positioning, 77–78. *See also* Repositioning
Postindustrial society, 5
Pratt and Whitney, 207
Preservatives, 79
Price:
    competition, 20, 77, 125, 173. *See also* Pricing strategy
    and convenience, 103
    loss, 166
    raising, 9
    value, 115
Price gap, 72
Price–performance ratio, *see* Performance-price ratio
Price protection, 174
Price war, 177, 178
Pricing strategy, 141–142, 144, 167, 180, 213, 228. *See also* Price, competition
Printing technology, 145
Privatization, 24
Procter and Gamble, 160
Product development, 100, 101, 109, 139, 158, 169, 185, 199
Product enhancement, 200
Product failure, 76
Product innovation, 21
Production, 145
Production cost, 77, 166, 174, 227
Production efficiency, 167
Production facilities, 143, 187
Production volume, 165, 171, 173
Productivity, 17–18, 22, 220

Product obsolescence, 211
Product safety, 21, 50, 51, 185
Product/service benefits, 6, 220
Profit, 5
Profitability, 139, 158, 166, 213
Profit margins, 133
Profit squeeze, 20
Promotion, 59, 76
Prudential Insurance, 29
Psychological blocks, 84–94, 99, 178
    image barrier, 90–94, 99
    tradition barrier, 84–90, 99
Public assistance programs, 117
Publicity, 59
Public relations, 38
Public safety, 12
Public Utility Commission (PUC), 51
Pull marketing, 59, 223
Purchasing hours, 13

Quaker Oats, 180
Quality, 91
Quality assurance, 23–24, 220
Quality circles, 23, 85
Quality of life, 135
Quality standards, 48

Rate regulation, 51
RCA, 38, 73, 224
Redistribution:
    of income, 13
    of time, 12–13
Regulation barrier:
    cellular phones, 125
    custom calling services, 133
    digital centrex, 119–120
    as environmental challenge, 50–55, 99
    food industry, 79
    lifeline services, 114
    oral contraceptives, 148
    self-regulation, 50, 222
    software development, 188
    telecommunications industry, 105–106, 110
    thermography, 185
    toll-free services, 129
    videotex, 101
Regulations, 6, 21, 211
    as barrier to innovation, 31
    changing, 24–26, 218, 221

Index

Regulatory climate, 101
Regulatory problems, 147
Regulatory uncertainty, 145
Relative value, 77
Reorganization, 54
Repositioning, 193, 224. See also Positioning
Research alliances, 37–38, 221
Research and development (R&D):
   alliances, 37
   cellular phones, 124
   cost, 180, 227
   at DuPont, 145
   facilities, 207, 233
   at IBM, 157, 209
   operations barrier, 39
   specialization trap, 31
   telecommunications industry, 104
Resistance (to change), 39, 66–94, 98, 110, 122, 146, 156, 183, 189, 207, 213, 218, 225, 234. See also Barriers
Resource allocation, 101
Resource barrier:
   cellular phones, 124–125
   custom calling services, 133
   digital centrex, 119
   electronic mail, 109–119
   as environmental challenge, 44–50, 99, 222
   lifeline services, 114
   microwave ovens, 147
   soft drink industry, 169
   telecommunications industry, 105
   toll-free services, 129
Resources (financial), 31, 101, 186, 227
Respect, 87–88
Retailing, 48, 219
Retirement, 11
Reynolds, R.J., 38, 56
Risk, 78, 79, 80, 127, 131, 143, 190
Risk aversion, 80
Risk avoidance, 80, 166
Risk barrier, 78–79, 99, 224
   cellular phones, 127
   custom calling services, 135
   digital centrex, 121–122
   electronic mail, 111
   lifeline services, 116
   microwave ovens, 147
   oral contraceptives, 148
   telecommunications industry, 107

thermography, 186
toll-free services, 131
videotex, 103
Robotics, 43, 67, 222, 223

Safety, 12, 21, 50, 51, 185
Safety devices, 63
Safety standards, 26, 51, 221
Satellite Business Systems, 110, 161
Satellite communications, 209
Satellite technology, 29
Savin, 83, 85
Scarcities, 21
Searle, G.D., 179, 231
Sears, 38, 41, 58, 76, 83, 221
Security, personal, 7, 12, 219
Seiko, 77, 167
Self-protection, 12
Self-regulation, 50, 222
Selling, 42, 48
Separate operations, 42, 222
Service, 42, 48
Services sector, 5, 52, 68, 81
Sharp Corporation, 47
Siemens, 33, 45, 105
Singapore, 56, 89
Single-person households, 14–16, 219
Skunk works, 5, 35, 38, 42, 221
Slow and Steady strategy, 141–164, 227–229
Smart house project, 37, 48, 222
Snap-on-Tools, 48
Social security, 11, 170, 219
Soft drink industry, 55, 169–170, 172, 223
Software development, 187–188, 191–192, 195, 232
Software Publishing Corporation, 192
Sony Corporation, 47
Soup, 69, 78, 224
Spain, 171, 229
Specialization, 32–33, 34, 100
Specialization trap, 31–44
   expertise barrier, 31, 32–39
   operations barrier, 31, 39–44
Stand-alone business, 124
Standard Oil Company, 50, 162
Standards:
   quality, 48
   safety, 26, 51, 221
   technical, 25–26, 221

Steel industry, 32, 144, 152, 221
Stereotypes, 91, 92, 99, 103, 135, 225
Stigmas, 91
Strategic alliances, 21, 100, 105
Structural dysfunction, 30
Subaru, 175
Sumitomo, 45
Supreme Court, 54
Survey research methods, 65
Switzerland, 55
Synthetic turf, 186–187
System packaging, 83–84, 224
Systems perspective, 70, 223
Systems selling, 211–212, 234

Taboos, 91, 99, 187, 225
Taiwan, 56, 91
Tandy Corporation, 80, 158
Tariffs, 21, 56, 133
Tax laws, 10, 11
Technical expertise, 157, 186, 208
Technical specialization, 32–33, 34
Technical standards, 25–26, 221
Technical versatility, 32
Technocrats, 35
Technological breakthroughs, 6, 16–19, 157, 208, 218, 219–220, 233
Technological developments, 4, 39
Technological evolution, 25
Technological innovations, 86, 161, 213
Technology, ages of, 17–19
Technology-driven innovation, 33, 98, 213
Technology transfer, 21, 220
Telecommunications, 21, 49, 71
Telecommunications industry:
　deregulation, 173
　integration, 71
　measurement procedures, 97, 225–226
　monopolies, 64–65
　rate regulation, 51
　reorganization, 54
　resource barriers, 46
　technical standards, 25, 221
Telecommunications network, 104, 146
Telecommunications technology, 157
Teleconferencing, 68, 74, 161, 224
Telemarketing, 58
Television, 155, 158
Television programming, 15, 29, 158, 219
Testimonials, 82–83, 156, 224

Testing, 70, 79, 145, 156, 171, 229
Texas Instruments, 167, 171–172, 174, 175–178, 197, 229, 230
Thermography, 81, 185, 190–191, 195, 231
Third World countries, 56, 86–87, 91, 148, 155
Tide detergent, 76
Time:
　convenience, 72, 103
　discretionary, 12–13
　efficiency, 111
　redistribution of, 12–13
　value, 103, 126, 155
Time management, 13
Time and motion studies, 22
Time-poor society, 13
Timex, 77, 167
Tofu, 69
Toll-free services, 128–132, 137
Toyota, 21, 175, 220
Trade barriers, 21, 56, 220, 223
Trademarks, 51
Trade practices, 50
Tradition barrier:
　cellular phones, 127
　custom calling services, 135
　digital centrex, 122
　electronic mail, 112
　lifeline services, 116–117
　oral contraceptives, 148
　as psychological block, 84–90, 99, 224
　telecommunications industry, 107–108
　thermography, 186
　toll-free services, 131
　videotex, 103
Training:
　customer, 134, 188
　worker, 23, 39, 68, 99, 110, 126, 211, 222
Transportation, Department of, 205
Trial and error, 70, 122
Trickle-down theory, 90
Tupperware, 58, 225
Tylenol, 76
Typewriters, see Electronic typewriters

Underwriters Laboratory (UL), 185
Unions, 24, 85
United Airlines, 88
United Satellite Communications (USCI), 29–30

Index

United States Postal Service, 109
United Telephone, 46
Universal products, 22
Upstreaming, 43
Usage, 145
Usage barrier, 66–71, 99, 223
    cellular phones, 126
    custom calling services, 134
    digital centrex, 121
    electronic mail, 110–111
    lifeline services, 115
    Slow and Steady strategy, 143
    telecommunications industry, 106–107
    toll-free services, 130
    videotex, 102
Usage patterns, 203
U.S. Sprint, 46, 172, 173, 211

Value, 76, 141, 143, 224
    creating, 3, 9
    relative, 77
    in world markets, 23
Value-added features, 107
Value-added services, 132, 133, 211
Value barrier, 71–78, 99, 224
    cellular phones, 126–127
    custom calling services, 134–135
    digital centrex, 121
    electronic mail, 111
    lifeline services, 115–116
    telecommunications services, 107
    toll-free services, 130–131
    videotex, 102–103

Value progression, 141
Vasectomy, 159–160
VCRs, 47, 59, 73
Vectra International Corporation, 190, 195, 196, 231
Venture capital, 49–50, 222
Versatility, 17–18, 32, 220
Video cameras, 80
Video disks, 73–74, 204, 224
Videotex, 27, 37, 70, 90, 99–104, 137, 157, 221
Vision systems, 43
Volkswagen, 34, 188, 196
Vulnerability, 6

Wage structures, 24
Wang, 85, 89
Warner Communications, 177
Warranties, 79
Watches, 77, 167
Wealth preservation, 7, 10–12, 219
Westinghouse, 41
Whirlpool, 38, 41
Wine industry, 40, 94
Work flow, 23, 66, 107, 143, 223
World Health Organization (WHO), 88–89
World market, 20, 23

Xerox, 32, 85, 89, 159, 228

Yuppies, 90

Zenith Corporation, 67

```
658.578 S554b

Sheth, Jagdish N.

Bringing innovation to
 market
```